PLANETARY SCIENCE

EXPLORE NEW FRONTIERS

Matthew Brenden Wood
Illustrated by Sam Carbaugh

Nomad Press
A division of Nomad Communications
10 9 8 7 6 5 4 3 2 1

This book was manufactured by Versa Press
East Peoria, Illinois
September 2017, Job # J17-06478

ISBN Softcover: 978-1-61930-571-7
ISBN Hardcover: 978-1-61930-567-0

Educational Consultant, Marla Conn

Questions regarding the ordering of this book should be addressed to
Nomad Press
2456 Christian St.
White River Junction, VT 05001
www.nomadpress.net

Printed in the United States.

More science titles in the
Inquire and Investigate series

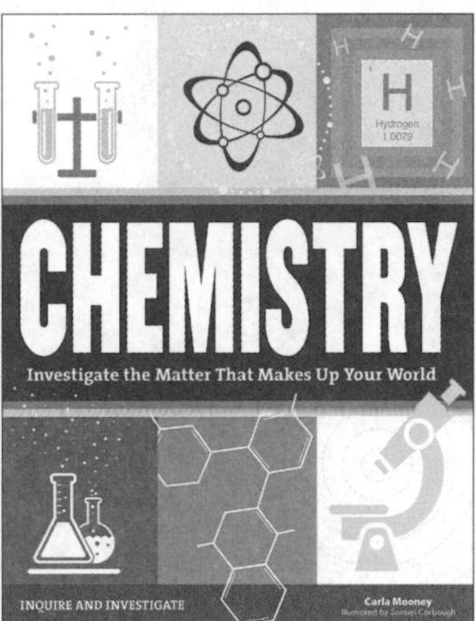

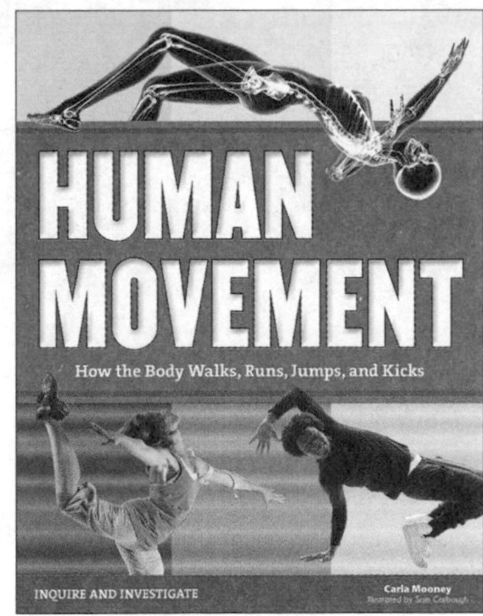

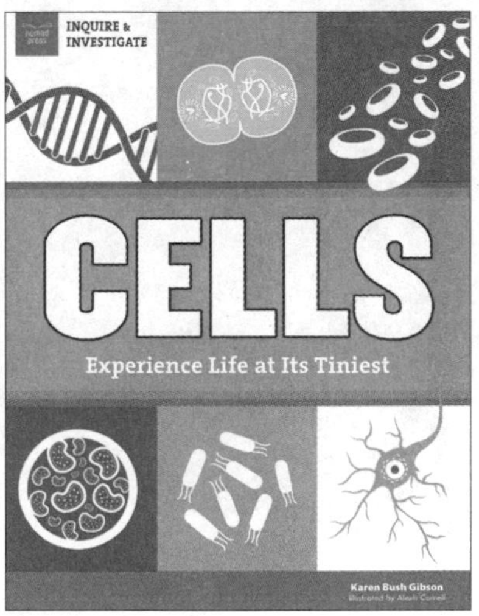

Check out more titles at www.nomadpress.net

You can use a smartphone or tablet app to scan the QR codes and explore more! Cover up neighboring QR codes to make sure you're scanning the right one. You can find a list of URLs on the Resources page.

If the QR code doesn't work, try searching the Internet with the Keyword Prompts to find other helpful sources.

 Planets

Contents

VENUS

Discovery Date: Unknown

Discovered by: Ancient Peoples

Distance from Sun: 0.723 AU

Length of Year: 224.7 Earth Days

Length of Day: 224.65 Earth Days

Mass: 0.815 Earths

Diameter: 7,521 Miles (12,104 Kilometers)

Gravity: 0.907 times Earth Gravity

Atmosphere: Carbon Dioxide

Moons: None

MARS

Discovery Date: Unknown

Discovered by: Ancient Peoples

Distance from Sun: 1.52 AU

Length of Year: 687 Earth Days

Length of Day: 24.7 Hours

Mass: 0.107 Earths

Diameter: 4,220 Miles (6,792 Kilometers)

Gravity: 0.377 times Earth Gravity

Atmosphere: Carbon Dioxide

Moons: 2

JUPITER

Discovery Date: Unknown

Discovered by: Ancient Peoples

Distance from Sun: 5.2 AU

Length of Year: 11.9 Earth Years

Length of Day: 9.9 Hours

Mass: 317.8 Earths

Diameter: 88,846 Miles (142,984 Kilometers)

Gravity: 2.36 times Earth Gravity

Atmosphere: Hydrogen, Helium

Known Moons: About 67

You are here.

MERCURY

Discovery Date: Unknown

Discovered by: Ancient Peoples

Distance from Sun: 0.387 AU

Length of Year: 88 Earth Days

Length of Day: 58.6 Earth Days

Mass: 0.050 Earths

Diameter: 3,032 Miles (4,879 Kilometers)

Gravity: 0.378 times Earth Gravity

Atmosphere: Traces of Hydrogen, Helium, Oxygen

Moons: None

EARTH

Discovery Date: Unknown

Discovered by: Ancient Peoples

Distance from Sun: 1 AU

Length of Year: 365 Earth Days

Length of Day: 24 Hours

Mass: 5,973,600,000,000,000,000,000,000 Kilograms

Diameter: 7,926 Miles (12,756 Kilometers)

Gravity: 1: Earth Gravity

Atmosphere: Nitrogen, Oxygen

Moons: 1

CERES

Discovery Date: 1801

Discovered by: Giuseppe Piazzi

Distance from Sun: 30.1 AU

Length of Year: 4.6 Earth Years

Length of Day: 5.34 Hours

Mass: 0.00015 Earths

Diameter: 326 Miles (525 Kilometers)

Gravity: 0.028 times Earth Gravity

Atmosphere: Traces of Water Vapor

Moons: None

KEY

1 AU = About 93 Million Miles (149,598,000 Kilometers)

NEPTUNE

Discovery Date: 1846

Discovered by: Le Verrier, Adams, Galle

Distance from Sun: 30.1 AU

Length of Year: 163.7 Earth Years

Length of Day: 16.1 Hours

Mass: 17.1 Earths

Diameter: 30,775 Miles (49,528 Kilometers)

Gravity: 1.12 times Earth Gravity

Atmosphere: Hydrogen, Helium

Known Moons: About 14

PLUTO

Discovery Date: 1930

Discovered by: Clyde Tombaugh

Distance from Sun: 29.7–49.3 AU

Length of Year: 249 Earth Years

Length of Day: 6.38 Earth Days

Mass: 0.0022 Earths

Diameter: 1,473 Miles (2,370 Kilometers)

Gravity: 0.063 Times Earth Gravity

Atmosphere: Nitrogen

Moons: 5

SATURN

Discovery Date: Unknown

Discovered by: Ancient Peoples

Distance from Sun: 9.58 AU

Length of Year: 29.4 Earth Years

Length of Day: 10.7 Hours

Mass: 95.2 Earths

Diameter: 74,898 Miles (120,536 Kilometers)

Gravity: 0.916 times Earth Gravity

Atmosphere: Hydrogen, Helium

Known Moons: About 62

URANUS

Discovery Date: 1781

Discovered by: William Herschel

Distance from Sun: 19.2 AU

Length of Year: 83.7 Earth Years

Length of Day: 17.2 Hours

Mass: 14.5 Earths

Diameter: 31,763 Miles (51,118 Kilometers)

Gravity: 0.889 times Earth Gravity

Atmosphere: Hydrogen, Helium

Known Moons: About 27

NOTE: Drawings of planets in this book are not to scale.

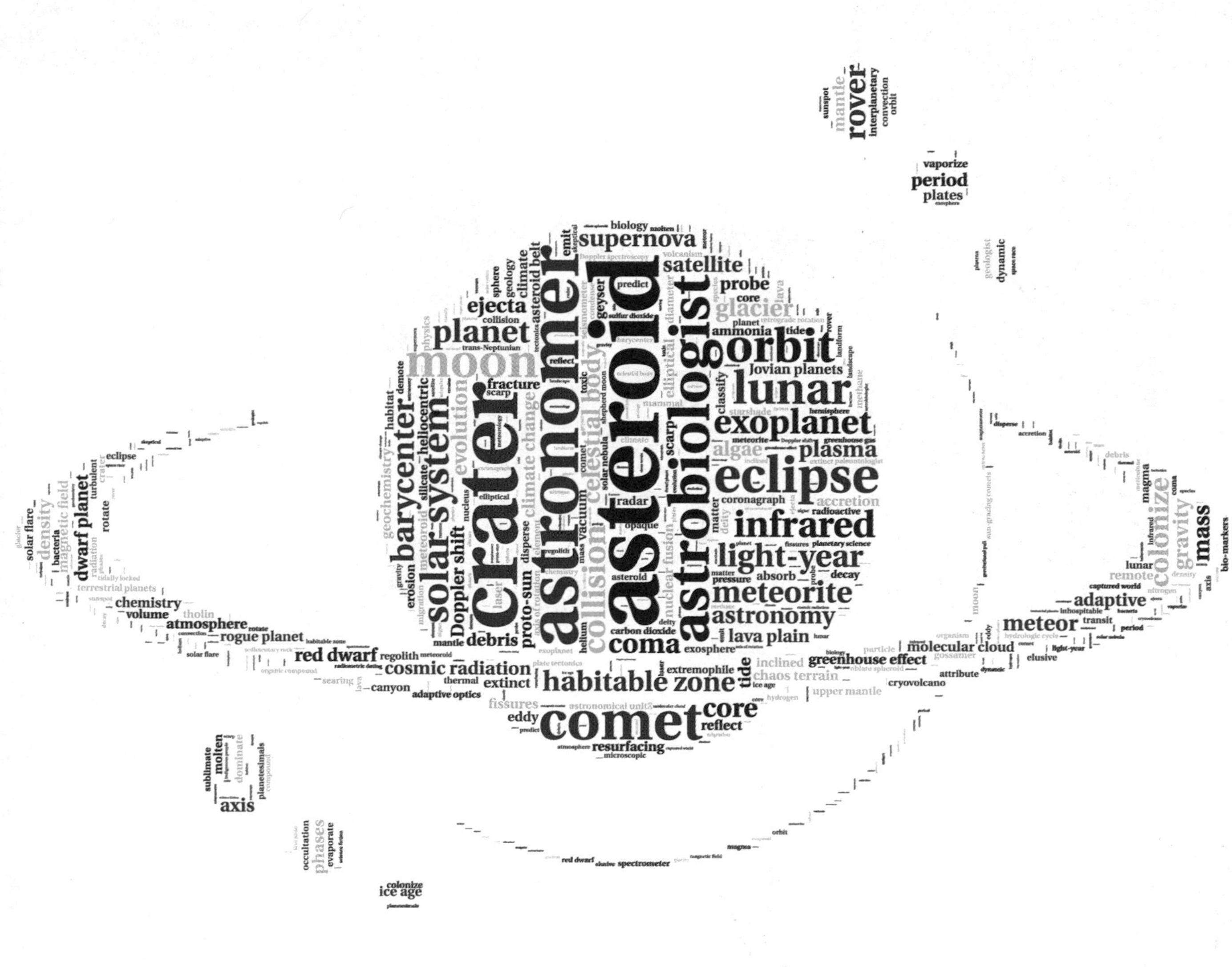

Introduction

Studying Other Planets

What is planetary science?

Planetary science is the scientific study of planets, moons, asteroids, comets, and other objects in the solar system. To study these objects, planetary scientists use many different areas of science, such as astronomy, chemistry, physics, meteorology, and geology.

If you go outside on a clear night and look up, you might be able to see one or more planets. Mercury, Venus, Mars, Jupiter, and Saturn are all visible from our own planet, Earth. What are these celestial objects? Why is it important to learn about them?

Planetary scientists work to understand what planets are made of, what characteristics they share, and how they are different. They study the history of planets and their behaviors. These scientists search for answers to questions that people have had about planets since humans first looked up in the sky.

About 4.6 billion years ago, our solar system was new. It was nothing more than a huge cloud of swirling hydrogen gas, dust, and ice particles called a molecular cloud. Created from the violent death of an ancient star called a supernova, the giant cloud stretched a few light-years across, slowly churning in space.

Gradually, the grains of dust and wisps of gas began to clump together. The clumps grew larger as their gravities pulled in more material.

In the hot, dense center of the cloud, a proto-sun formed. The rest of the cloud formed a swirling disk around it called the solar nebula. Inside the solar nebula, microscopic particles of dust and ice continued to move about, sometimes colliding and sticking together.

During the course of millions of years, this process, called accretion, formed objects a few miles across. These objects are called planetesimals, and they are the building blocks of planets. As millions more years passed, these planetesimals collided and merged with each other. Among the debris, only a few remained.

Today, our solar system consists of eight planets and their moons, dwarf planets, asteroids, and comets. Planetary science is the study of these objects, and it involves many different branches of science working together to try to answer some very big questions.

Where did these objects come from? Why are some of them so similar and others so different? Is our solar system unique?

VOCAB LAB

There is a lot of new vocabulary in this book! Turn to the glossary in the back when you come to a word you don't understand. Practice your new vocabulary in the **VOCAB LAB** activities in each chapter.

Scientific Method

The scientific method is the process scientists use to ask questions and find answers. Keep a science journal to record your methods and observations during all the activities in this book. You can use a scientific method worksheet to keep your ideas and observations organized.

Question: What are we trying to find out? What problem are we trying to solve?

Research: What is already known about this topic?

Hypothesis: What do we think the answer will be?

Equipment: What supplies are we using?

Method: What procedure are we following?

Results: What happened and why?

WHAT'S A PLANET?

What do you consider to be a planet? Does it need to be a certain size or shape? Surprisingly, there wasn't a real definition of a planet until 2006. That's when the International Astronomical Union (IAU), an organization that determines names for objects in space, faced a problem.

Astronomers had recently found several objects orbiting farther from the sun than the planet Pluto. In fact, one of them was thought to be larger than Pluto itself. And astronomers estimated that many more objects like Pluto might be hiding in the outer solar system. Without a real definition, they reasoned, we might end up with more planets than we could name.

In order to keep this from happening, the IAU settled on the following requirements for planet-hood. A planet must:

- orbit the sun;
- be massive enough that its gravity pulls itself into a round, or nearly round, shape; and
- have cleared its neighborhood of other objects.

This definition also made a big change to the solar system—Pluto was no longer a planet, but a dwarf planet. Pluto met the first two requirements, but not the third. Because of its small size, it wasn't able to clear away other objects in its neighborhood.

However, Pluto wasn't alone in being affected by the new definition. Ceres, once considered the largest asteroid, was now a dwarf planet. Newly discovered objects beyond Pluto, such as Eris, Makemake, and Haumea, were also categorized as dwarf planets.

The planets in our solar system are usually separated into two groups—the inner planets and the outer planets. The inner planets, also called terrestrial planets, are smaller, rockier worlds with solid surfaces. The outer planets, sometimes called Jovian planets, are larger and made mostly of gases.

Starting from the sun, the inner planets Mercury, Venus, Earth, and Mars are followed by the dwarf planet Ceres. Next comes the asteroid belt, which separates the inner planets from the outer planets Jupiter, Saturn, Uranus, and Neptune. Beyond Neptune are the trans-Neptunian objects. These include Pluto and the other dwarf planets of the outer solar system.

Even farther beyond the trans-Neptunian family lies the Oort Cloud, where icy comets are thought to come from.

Not everyone was a fan of Pluto's reclassification from planet to dwarf planet status. Do you think the IAU made the right call?

STUDYING PLANETARY SCIENCE

PRIMARY SOURCES

Primary sources come from people who were eyewitnesses to events. They might write about the event, take pictures, post short messages to social media or blogs, or record the event for radio or video. Why are primary sources important? Do you learn differently from primary sources than from secondary sources, which come from people who did not directly experience the event?

There are a few terms that are important to know to study planets. They'll help you understand some of the amazing facts about planets and their environments!

All of the objects in the solar system follow a path called an orbit. All planets, dwarf planets, comets, and asteroids orbit the sun, while moons, also called satellites, orbit these bodies. The amount of time it takes a planet to complete one orbit around the sun is called its period, or year. The farther a planet is from the sun, the longer its year will be.

All planets spin around an axis of rotation—the time it takes to make one rotation is called a day. For example, it takes 24 hours for Earth to complete one rotation around its axis, giving us our 24-hour day.

> Before the invention of the telescope, most astronomers believed the planets were points of light that moved against a background of stationary stars.

In 1608, Hans Lippershey (1570–1619) was the first person to apply for a patent for a telescope. However, it's not known if he was the first person to build one.

Galileo Galilei's (1564–1642) first observations of the planets through a simple telescope changed astronomy forever. Many historians consider this to be the beginning of planetary science. However, even before the invention of the telescope, astronomers such as Johannes Kepler (1571–1630) and Nicolaus Copernicus (1473–1543) discovered a great deal about the planets and their motions through the sky. They used careful observation and mathematical reasoning to make their discoveries.

Johannes Kepler discovered the laws of planetary motion, describing how the planets move through their orbits. And Copernicus was a champion of the heliocentric model of the solar system, arguing that the sun, not Earth, is at its center.

Modern planetary scientists have an incredible number of tools with which to study celestial objects. Telescopes, satellites, space probes, and robotic rovers have given us knowledge of the solar system that was impossible less than a century ago. Who knows what tools we might develop in the future and what we'll discover with them?

In *Planetary Science: Explore New Frontiers*, you'll investigate the objects in our solar system and beyond by examining what makes each unique. You'll learn not only their fascinating properties, but also the exciting history of their exploration, from the first time each was observed through a telescope to the most recent close-up images.

You will also explore some of the most important questions planetary science has set out to answer. Is Earth the only planet capable of supporting life? Is Planet 9 hiding at the edge of the solar system? Will we ever find an Earth-like planet in a solar system other than our own? In planetary science, what we don't know can be even more exciting than what we do know.

KEY QUESTIONS

- **Why is it important to study other planets?**
- **How can we learn about events that took place more than 4 billion years ago?**

VOCAB LAB 

Write down what you think each word means. What root words can you find that will help?

proto-sun, **solar nebula**, **accretion**, **planetesimal**, **terrestrial**, **Jovian**, **orbit**, **axis of rotation**, **rotate**, and **heliocentric**.

Compare your definitions with those of your friends or classmates. Did you all come up with the same meanings? Turn to the text and glossary if you need help.

Inquire & Investigate

CAN YOU SPOT MERCURY?

Although it's one of the brightest objects in the sky, seeing the closest planet to the sun isn't easy. As seen from Earth, it never strays far from the sun's blinding glare. Many famous astronomers are rumored to have never seen the elusive planet.

Caution: Never look at the sun through binoculars or a telescope.

- **To see Mercury, you need to catch it at either dawn or dusk at just the right time of year.** Even then, it isn't easy to see. Use this website to determine when Mercury is visible to you.

  naked eye planets

- **You'll need a clear view of the horizon.** Gazing from a hilltop or tall building is helpful. Wait until the sun has set or just before it rises.
- **If you choose to use binoculars or a telescope to observe, NEVER LOOK AT THE SUN.** It can permanently damage your eyes. Pointing a telescope or binoculars at the sun can even start a fire. Always be safe!
- **Record your observations during several days in a row.** Here are some questions to think about.

  1. How does Mercury's position change from night to night?
  2. Does Mercury's brightness appear to change?
  3. Once Mercury is no longer visible, how long do you think it will take before it reappears? Will it show up in the morning or evening sky?

To investigate more, ask a friend or family member who lives far away for help. Have them record their observations of Mercury and compare results. Are they different? Why or why not?

Chapter 1

The Hot Planets: Mercury and Venus

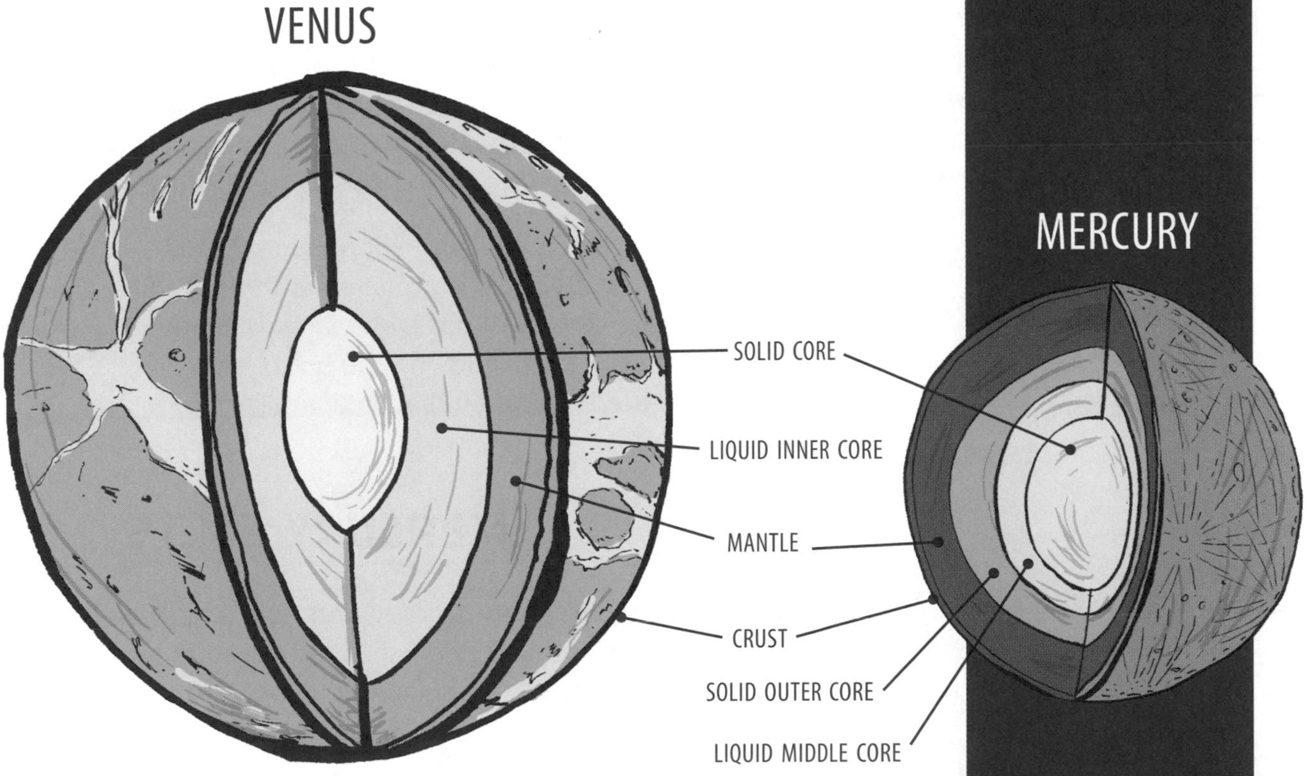

VENUS

MERCURY

SOLID CORE

LIQUID INNER CORE

MANTLE

CRUST

SOLID OUTER CORE

LIQUID MIDDLE CORE

Are Mercury and Venus hot for the same reasons?

As the closest planets to the sun, Mercury and Venus both have extremely hot temperatures that can make exploring them very difficult—but not impossible.

Mercury and Venus were both spotted by ancient humans in ancient times, but it wasn't until recently that scientists learned much about either of these warm worlds. The closest planets to the sun, these devastatingly hot planets have a natural defense system in the form of super-hot surfaces, making these worlds difficult to explore.

However, the things we do to learn about each planet might enable us to better help our planet Earth. Through climate change, the surface of our own planet is heating up. What can we learn from studying the hot planets about balancing the atmosphere and keeping Earth healthy?

MERCURY FACTS

Mercury is one of the least understood and least explored planets in the solar system, but not because it's uninteresting. Mercury is a fascinating planet of extremes.

Mercury is the fastest and smallest of the planets and is second only to Venus in its searing surface temperature.

For thousands of years, ancient cultures watched this speedy planet rise and set with sun. The Greeks had two names for the swift world, even though they knew they were the same object. When seen in the morning, it was called Apollo, the god of light. In the evening, it was called Hermes, the messenger god. The Romans named it Mercury after their own fleet-footed messenger god, and it's Mercury that we use today.

Mercury is the closest planet to the sun. At an average distance of 36 million miles, it's nearly three times as close to the sun as Earth and takes just 88 Earth days to complete one year. As you might guess, being that close to the sun means that the surface of Mercury can get extremely hot—the daytime temperature on Mercury can reach an incredible 806 degrees Fahrenheit (430 degrees Celsius). But Mercury can be very cold, too. Temperatures on Mercury's night side can drop to a frigid -292 degrees Fahrenheit (-180 degrees Celsius).

On Earth, a thick atmosphere helps to spread heat around the globe, but Mercury has only an exosphere. This is a very thin, wispy envelope of helium gas incapable of dispersing much of the heat. And the hot days and cold nights on Mercury are very, very long. It takes almost 59 Earth days to make just one day on Mercury—its day is two-thirds as long as its year!

Ancient Observations

For centuries, many cultures recorded detailed observations of Mercury's movements through the sky, but only in the last 50 years have we learned even the most basic facts about this fascinating and mysterious world.

SPACE ELEMENT

Mercury rotates on its axis three times for every two orbits around the sun. This means there are three Mercury days for every two Mercury years.

Although Mercury is the smallest planet in the solar system with a diameter of 3,032 miles, it's surprisingly massive. It has the second-highest density, after Earth. This means that even though its diameter is only slightly larger than the moon, you would weigh twice as much on Mercury as you would on the lunar surface.

THE LEAST-EXPLORED PLANET

Most of what we know about Mercury was discovered in just the last 60 years. Even the length of Mercury's day was unknown until 1965. Using Earth-based radar, scientists discovered that instead of keeping one side always facing the sun as they had suspected, Mercury actually experienced day and night. And it wasn't until 1974 that planetary scientists got a good look at the surface when *Mariner 10* became the first spacecraft to fly by Mercury.

The first pictures from *Mariner 10* showed an ancient planet covered in mountains, dried-up lava plains, and craters of all sizes, very similar to the moon. Although it only made three passes by Mercury, *Mariner 10* managed to photograph nearly half of the surface and discovered that Mercury has a very weak but measurable magnetic field, as well as a faint exosphere made mostly of helium.

After *Mariner 10*'s brief encounter, Mercury wasn't visited again until 2008, when the *MESSENGER* probe arrived to fully map and uncover more of the planet's secrets.

WHAT IS A MAGNETIC FIELD?

Magnetic fields act like huge bar magnets deep inside planets. In the case of rocky planets such as Mercury, the planet's rotation causes the iron core to spin, generating an electric current and creating a magnetic field. Mercury's magnetic field is 100 times weaker than Earth's.

A HOT, SHRINKING PLANET—WITH ICE

One of the most surprising findings made by *MESSENGER* was that Mercury joins Earth as the only known tectonically active planets in the solar system. The discovery of young fault scarps, which are long, cliff-like landforms, appear to show where Mercury's surface, or crust, is broken and pushed upwards. It's thought that as Mercury cools and contracts from its formation, the crust is pushed together, causing huge stretches of the surface to be lifted up to look like a long stair-step. Some of these scarps are hundreds of miles long!

Perhaps the most amazing discovery made by *MESSENGER* were observations that supported the hypothesis of the presence of water on Mercury in the form of ice. Although Mercury experiences the hottest temperatures in the solar system, *MESSENGER* found evidence that ice might exist in just the right places. Using several different instruments, including radar, the spacecraft detected signs of frozen water in spots where the sun never shines—the craters at Mercury's poles.

MESSENGER is an acronym that stands for MErcury Surface, Space ENvironment, GEochemistry, and Ranging.

PS

Mercury's southern hemisphere

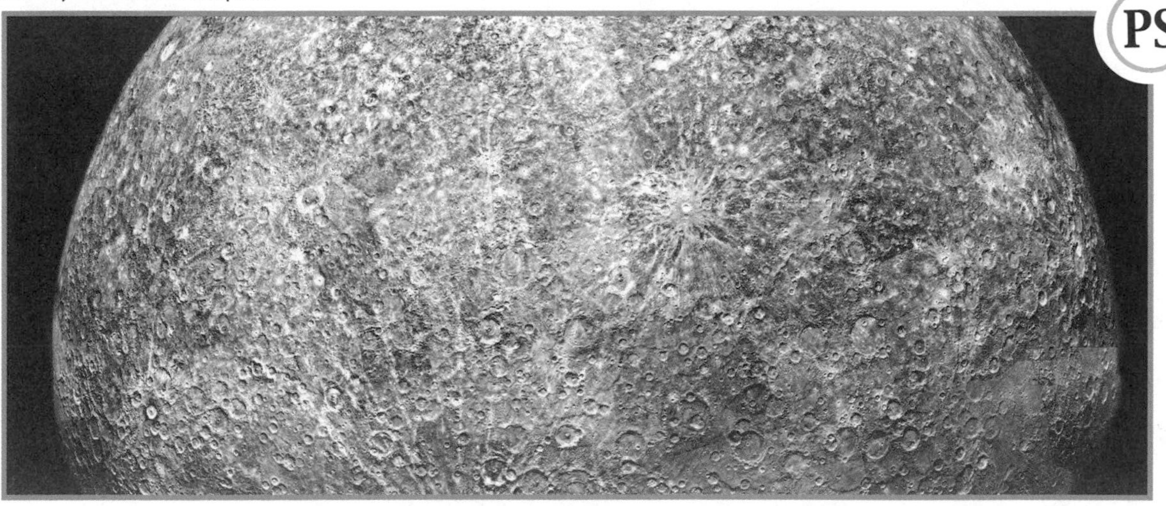

photo credit: NOAA

If you were to stand at Mercury's North Pole, the sun would always appear at the very edge of the horizon, creating long shadows across the heavily cratered landscape. If you stepped inside one of those craters, you would find areas that are always in darkness. And with no significant atmosphere to spread heat around, the temperature in the shade is extremely cold, allowing water to remain frozen. In these places, ice can exist for millions of years without disappearing.

With *MESSENGER*, scientists were able to make incredible discoveries and collect lots of data, but *MESSENGER* couldn't last forever. With its last drops of fuel, it was steered into a collision course with Mercury, making a new crater and ending its exploration in April 2015.

Planetary scientists think that the ice likely came from comets crashing into Mercury during a period of solar system formation called the "heavy bombardment." This was a time when the inner planets were pummeled by comets from the outer edge of the solar system. The only ice that remains are the deposits that sit in permanent darkness.

WHAT'S NEXT FOR MERCURY?

Even though *Mariner 10* and *MESSENGER* returned large amounts of information, their discoveries have led scientists to ask even more questions. Is Mercury's core solid or liquid? Why is Mercury's magnetic field so weak? What can Mercury tell us about the early formation of the solar system?

In 2018, the European Space Agency (ESA) and Japan Aerospace Exploration Agency (JAXA) plan to launch *BepiColombo*. This spacecraft is actually two probes in one: the Mercury Planetary Orbiter (MPO) and the Mercury Magnetosphere Orbiter (MMO). The MPO will analyze the surface and internal structure of the planet, while the MMO will closely monitor Mercury's weak magnetic field. It's expected to arrive at Mercury in 2026, after making a few short visits to Venus.

VENUS FACTS

Venus might be the strangest of all the inner planets. On one hand, it's often described as Earth's twin. Both planets are nearly the same size and mass and have similar compositions. But the similarities stop there. Venus has a super-dense atmosphere, toxic rain, and surface temperatures hot enough to melt lead.

Venus is the only planet named for a female deity. All of the other planets are named for male gods.

The Romans called the wandering star Venus, after their goddess of love.

When it's at its brightest, Venus is the most brilliant light in the sky, leading ancient people to give it names that described its beauty. But beneath Venus's brilliant cloud tops lies a very inhospitable world.

With a diameter of 7,521 miles and a mass just 18 percent less than Earth, the two planets seem similar at first glance. Even the force of gravity at Venus's surface is nearly the same as Earth's. Venus is the second planet from the sun, orbiting at an average distance of 67 million miles. Being closer to the sun means a shorter year. A Venusian year lasts about 225 Earth days. But to experience one full day on Venus it would take nearly 243 Earth days—a day on Venus is longer than its year!

It's thought that Venus was struck by a large object soon after its formation, causing it to tip over and spin in the "wrong" direction.

Unlike Mercury, Venus has an incredibly thick atmosphere, made mostly of carbon dioxide. Its atmosphere hides the planet's surface from above and allows only a small amount of sunlight to reach the ground. What might this feel like if we could stand on Venus's surface? The pressure from Venus's atmosphere is a crushing 92 times greater than what we feel on Earth. This thick atmosphere keeps the planet at a scorching 864 degrees Fahrenheit (462 degrees Celsius), even on the planet's night side!

Anyone unlucky enough to find themselves out in the open on Venus would be crushed and cooked by the carbon dioxide atmosphere in a very short amount of time.

Venus (and Uranus) rotate in the opposite direction, east to west, of all the other planets in the solar system. This is called retrograde rotation. On Venus, the pale glow of the sun rises very slowly in the west and sets in the east more than 121 Earth days later.

A Heliocentric World

The phases of Venus helped prove that the sun, not Earth, was at the center of the solar system. Read more here about Galileo and his struggle to prove to the world that Copernicus was right.

universe today Galileo

A HARD PLANET TO STUDY

Like Mercury, Venus is a difficult planet to study. In 1609, Galileo Galilei was the first astronomer to point a telescope at the planet. He discovered that Venus shows phases, just like the moon. But because the planet is always shrouded in bright, yellowish clouds, he was unable to learn much else. It wasn't until 1961, with the first radar measurements of Venus, that scientists finally knew the length of a Venusian day.

With the dawn of the space race in 1957, the Soviet Union and the United States each tried sending probes to Venus. In 1962, *Mariner 2* became the first successful inter-planetary mission.

The spacecraft measured Venus's surface temperature for the first time. It found that, unlike Earth, Venus lacks a strong magnetic field and has no water vapor in its atmosphere.

In 1990, the NASA spacecraft *Magellan* entered Venus's orbit and began mapping the planet beneath it. Because Venus's atmosphere is opaque to visible light, *Magellan* used radar to peep beneath the clouds and map more than 98 percent of the surface. The orbiter found that around 85 percent of Venus is covered in volcanic lava flows that give the planet a very smooth appearance.

Magellan's radar also found no small craters on Venus. Scientists think that the thick atmosphere helps to break up meteors before they can reach the surface.

Evidence gathered by *Magellan* and other spacecraft suggests that Venus once had water, much like the Earth does, but that water is long gone. Most planetary scientists believe that Venus's early volcanism released carbon dioxide gas into the atmosphere, helping to trap heat. As the temperatures around Venus rose, the water began to evaporate, adding water vapor to the atmosphere and trapping even more heat. This cycle eventually led to most of Venus's water evaporating into space. Left behind was a dry world wrapped in a dense envelope of carbon dioxide.

VENERA 9

The Soviet Union made no fewer than four attempts before finally parachuting *Venera 9* to the planet's surface in 1975. Despite the crushing atmosphere and intense heat, the probe managed to send back the first images from the surface of another planet before contact was lost after 53 minutes.

An image of the surface of Venus, created with a computer using photographs sent from the *Magellan* orbiter

photo credit: JPL/NASA

PS

Climate scientists look at Venus as a warning—if we don't stop adding carbon dioxide and other greenhouse gases to the atmosphere, Earth might end up like a true twin of Venus.

Because *Magellan* revealed Venus to have a relatively smooth and young surface, planetary scientists wondered if there might still be active volcanoes hidden beneath the clouds. In 2006, the ESA's *Venus Express* arrived to study the planet's atmosphere in detail and look for signs of active volcanism. The spacecraft discovered regions of the planet that were suddenly hotter and then much cooler than others, suggesting that lava might still be flowing today. *Venus Express* also found that lightning occurs in Venus's violent and turbulent atmosphere.

WHAT'S NEXT FOR VENUS?

With strong evidence that Venus might still be tectonically active, a new group of spacecraft was in the early stages of development to explore the planet in greater detail. NASA considered two ideas for the next visits to Venus. DAVINCI would explore the chemical composition of Venus's atmosphere by floating gently to the surface by parachute, much like the Soviet *Venera* spacecraft. It would search for evidence of volcanism by sniffing for sulfur dioxide in Venus's atmosphere.

VERITAS, a proposed orbiter, would orbit around the planet and use a variety of instruments to map the surface in greater detail. It would also trace the history of water on Venus and look for infrared signatures of erupting volcanoes and flowing lava. Both DAVINCI and VERITAS are on hold for now, and, instead, NASA may collaborate with Russia on another *Venera* mission. The mission could include an orbiter and a lander.

You might not suspect that right next door to the inhospitable hot planet lies the only planet in the solar system that we are sure supports life—our own planet Earth!

KEY QUESTIONS

- **What conditions contribute to the extreme heat on Mercury and Venus?**
- **Why do some scientists consider the greenhouse effect on Venus to be a warning for people on Earth?**

MAKE YOUR OWN CRATER

All the terrestrial planets have craters on their surface—even Earth! Craters are formed when an object or pieces of an object, such as an asteroid or comet, collide violently with a planet's surface. During an impact, material is thrown out from the crater and is known as ejecta. Some craters have large, mountain-like peaks at their center. Ejecta can sometimes look like rays, or lines, leading away from the center of the crater.

Caution: Be sure to wear eye protection.

- **Fill the pizza pan evenly with flour.** This will represent the fresh layer of planetary crust unearthed by your meteor. To create a darker surface layer on top of your planetary crust, sprinkle the chocolate cake mix until it covers the flour evenly.
- **Throw your meteor hard into your planetary crust!** What happens? Set up your planet surface again to repeat the experiment. Consider the following questions.
  - What determines the size and shape of your crater? Does it depend on the type of object you choose to use? Does it depend on the force you use to cause the impact?
  - How does changing the angle of your impact change the crater?
  - What happens if the flour is deeper or shallower? How does that affect the formation of your crater?

Ideas for Supplies

- eye protection
- aluminum pizza pan with an edge
- flour
- chocolate cake mix
- dry, clumpy soil or other meteor-like object

To investigate more, consider that many pictures of craters are taken when the sun is low on the horizon. This helps show the details of the crater itself by creating shadows. Try lighting your craters from different angles and taking pictures of the results. Can you create a picture that looks like the surface of Mercury or the moon?

Inquire & Investigate

VOCAB LAB

Write down what you think each word means. What root words can you find that will help?

exosphere, **disperse**, **magnetic field**, **tectonic**, **scarp**, **collision**, **toxic**, **retrograde rotation**, and **space race**.

Compare your definitions with those of your friends or classmates. Did you all come up with the same meanings? Turn to the text and glossary if you need help.

DISCOVERING DENSITY

With its huge metallic core, Mercury is the second-densest planet in the solar system. But how do scientists calculate density? Density is described as an object's mass per unit volume, or how tightly packed matter is in a certain amount of space. The density of an object can tell us a lot about that object.

- **Gather a number of objects together that are easy to measure.** Simple shapes are best, such as a brick or a baseball.
- **Calculate and record their volumes.** Here's a link to some volume equations for simple shapes.

 math tables volume

- **Weigh your objects and record your results.**
- **To calculate the density, divide an object's weight by its volume.** Consider the following questions.
  - How do different sizes and weights affect density?
  - What objects are the densest? Why do you think that is?
  - If an object can get wet, try placing it in water. Does it sink or float?
  - Compare the densities of objects that float to ones that don't. Can you determine at what density an object will float?

To investigate more, think about how you might measure the density of an oddly shaped object, such as a rock. How might you measure its volume? How did the ancient Greek Archimedes measure an object's volume?

Chapter 2

The Cool Planets: Earth and Mars

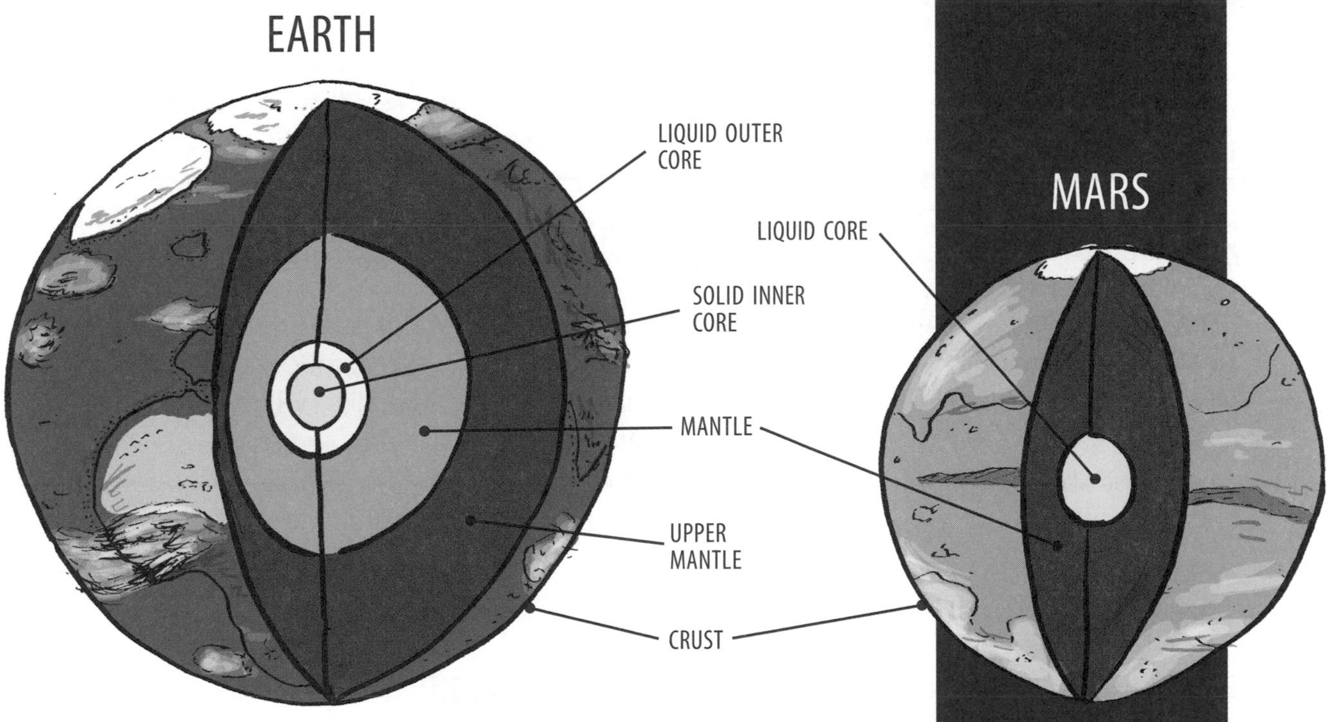

What are the similarities and differences between Earth and Mars?

Earth and Mars share many characteristics, which makes scientists hopeful that, someday, humans could travel to Mars and spend time on its surface. However, there are differences that present major challenges.

Earth and Mars are the two most-studied planets in the solar system. This is true for two very good reasons—one is where we live and the other is where we might go. Earth, home to an incredible number of plants and animals in its oceans and on its continents, is the only place in the solar system that has life.

Mars closely resembles much of our home world. Pictures of the red planet show a landscape of mountains, sand dunes, canyons, and polar ice caps, all of which can be found on both worlds. But while biologists have discovered life in even the most inhospitable places on Earth, we've yet to find any evidence of life on Mars.

Earth is our home. Everything that has ever happened in human history happened right here.

EARTH FACTS

Instead of being dry, cratered, or choked by toxic clouds, Earth is surrounded by a protective atmosphere that maintains the right temperatures and pressures needed to have oceans, lakes, and seas of water. It's home to millions of species of plants and animals, as well as bacteria, algae, and other forms of life. And this life survives pretty much everywhere we look—from the crushing pressures and superheated temperatures deep below the Earth's crust all the way to the freezing edge of the upper atmosphere. Because Earth seems to be the only planet with the right conditions for life, planetary scientists wonder: How did our planet turn out so different from the rest of the solar system?

With a diameter of 7,918 miles, Earth wins the title of largest terrestrial planet. Our home lies an average distance of 93 million miles from the sun, a distance astronomers call one astronomical unit. This places Earth comfortably inside the sun's habitable zone, or the region where the temperature is right for liquid water.

photo credit: NASA/JPL-Caltech/Space Science Institute

PALE BLUE DOT

"Look again at that dot. That's here. That's home. That's us. On it everyone you love, everyone you know, everyone you ever heard of, every human being who ever was, lived out their lives."
—Carl Sagan (1934–1996), scientist

Sometimes, we're treated to a new perspective of our planet. This photograph was taken from NASA's *Cassini* spacecraft as it flew near the rings of Saturn in the outer solar system. That's what our planet looks like from far, far away. Why is it important to see Earth from a distance? How might that view change our feelings and goals for our planet?

PS

Why do we have seasons? Check out the link below to learn more about how the tilt of Earth's axis brings us winter, spring, summer, and fall!

 universe today seasons

In its nearly circular orbit, Earth takes a little more than 365 days to complete one year, and a little less than 24 hours to complete one day. While Venus is tipped nearly upside-down, Earth's axis is tilted at a much less extreme 23.5 degrees, giving us our four seasons.

A substantial atmosphere provides a protective blanket for life on Earth, blocking harmful radiation and keeping the surface at a cozy average temperature of 54 degrees Fahrenheit (12 degrees Celsius). The strongest magnetic field of the four terrestrial worlds further protects the planet and its atmosphere from cosmic radiation, letting us enjoy a nice day at the beach with only the occasional sunburn to worry about. Earth also has one nearby satellite, one of the largest in the solar system—the moon.

The Habitable Zone

The habitable zone is a region around a star where the temperature is just right to allow water to remain a liquid on a planet's surface. Mars and Venus sit at the outer and inner edges of this zone, and don't have large amounts of water on their surfaces, as Earth does.

> The moon's gravitational pull causes ocean tides, and its beautiful phases help make nights a little less dark.

A COOL, WET WORLD

We know much more about Earth's history and makeup than the other planets simply because it's so much easier to study. For example, geologists can examine rocks and landforms in person, while meteorologists can monitor the atmosphere around the globe at any second. From orbit, satellites examine the planet, giving us new ways of seeing Earth. By understanding our own world, scientists can better understand the other planets and discover what makes them different.

Even from a distance, you can tell Earth is a unique place. The blue oceans, green and brown continents, and white clouds are found nowhere else in the solar system. Earth's protective atmosphere is about 249 miles thick, with most of it concentrated just 6 miles from the surface. Made of 78 percent nitrogen and 21 percent oxygen, it helps circulate water through the hydrologic cycle. As water evaporates from Earth's surface, it forms clouds that eventually release their moisture to fall back to the ground as rain or snow. Hurricanes and other intense storms help transport water and energy through the atmosphere, sometimes causing floods and even tornados.

The northern and southern hemispheres experience opposite seasons. When it's time to ice skate in Canada, people in Chile are hitting the beach!

An image of Earth from *Apollo 8*'s lunar orbit

photo credit: NASA

Climate Change

Earth's climate has changed dramatically in the past. Ice ages, followed by the thawing of glaciers, point to changes in temperature that sometimes caused mass migrations of life and even the extinction of millions of species of plants and animals. Today, scientists agree that Earth is warming again. This time, humans are extremely likely to be the dominant cause. In the last 150 years, people have been emitting more greenhouse gases into the atmosphere, allowing it to trap more heat from the sun. The results include the rapid melting of glaciers and polar caps, more dangerous weather patterns, and the destruction of habitats for many species. Scientists around the world are urging governments to take action now to protect the world from an unpredictable future.

Beneath the atmosphere, large continents and deep oceans cover the outermost layer of the planet. Instead of being one solid piece like Mercury and Venus, Earth's crust is made of several parts, called plates, that float on top of a somewhat molten upper mantle. These plates move slowly across the Earth's surface through a process called plate tectonics. For millions of years, they've slowly collided, split apart, and sunk under each other, creating the planet's landforms.

Earth's surface is almost completely free of craters, thanks to the process of erosion. For millions of years, plate tectonics, flowing water, and blowing winds have erased all but the largest and most recent craters. Together, these processes have shaped the oceans and continents, which are home to all kinds of life forms.

Below Earth's dynamic crust is the rocky mantle, which, at more than 1,800 miles thick, makes up most of the planet's mass. Below the mantle lies the core, which is divided into inner and outer layers of metals. The outer core is mostly liquid iron and nickel, and its motion is thought to be the source of Earth's strong magnetic field. At about 9,000 degrees Fahrenheit (5,000 degrees Celsius), the inner core is probably a sphere of iron and nickel, kept solid by the immense pressure from the layers above. All these features make Earth a perfect place for life. But how did Earth get this way?

A BRIEF HISTORY OF EARTH

Earth formed about 4.6 billion years ago from the same cloud of dust and gas as the other planets in the solar system. Scientists determined the age of the Earth using a process called radiometric dating. When rocks form, they contain radioactive elements that change or decay into different elements in very predictable ways.

By measuring how much of one element has changed into another, scientists can estimate the age of the rock. The oldest rocks on Earth are at least 4.4 billion years old, and figuring in the time it took to make them, scientists believe the Earth and the rest of the solar system formed together about 4.6 billion years ago.

At the time, proto-Earth's surface was covered in volcanoes and flowing lava, constantly bombarded by asteroids, comets, and even other proto-planets. Shortly after it formed, the Earth was struck by a proto-planet the size of Mars, which scooped out lots of material and created the moon.

As volcanoes belched gases from the Earth's molten interior, a poisonous atmosphere of carbon dioxide and ammonia slowly covered the planet's surface. By around 3.5 billion years ago, Earth had cooled enough to form a huge, salty ocean that covered most of its surface.

> It was in this ocean that the first bacteria-like organisms are thought to have appeared–the first life on Earth.

Another billion years later, blue-green algae appeared. The algae exhaled large amounts of oxygen into the air and changed the atmosphere dramatically.

Volcanoes and lava flows formed the first large land masses, creating continents that collided and split apart. Just 450 million years ago, life moved from the oceans onto land, and only 200 million years later, the first dinosaurs roamed. About 65 million years ago, a massive impact doomed the dinosaurs to extinction, allowing mammals, and eventually humans, to flourish.

Why is the Moon Covered in Craters?

When an object hits the moon at great speed, it tosses up huge amounts of material called ejecta. This material falls back to the moon, sometimes in long streaks called rays. Planetary scientists think that most of the moon's craters were formed between 3.8 and 3.9 billion years ago during the heavy bombardment. Check out this video to learn more about the evolution of the moon.

evolution moon NASA video

THE MOON

Being our closest celestial neighbor, the moon has always been a fascinating place to explore through telescopes, satellites, landers, and even by a dozen people. The Apollo space program landed astronauts on the moon six times between 1969 to 1972.

The fifth-largest satellite in the solar system and the largest satellite of the terrestrial planets, the moon is the only place in the solar system that humans have visited. With a diameter of 2,159 miles and orbiting Earth at an average distance of 148,417 miles, the moon is a big and familiar sight in the sky.

The moon is tidally locked with Earth, meaning it turns on its axis at the same rate that it orbits the Earth—every 27 days. This keeps the near side of the moon always facing Earth, and the other side, what scientists call the far side, always facing away. During a full moon, the entire near side is lit up by the sun, and during a new moon, only the far side is illuminated. In between the new and full moon, we see its different phases as it makes its way around the Earth.

The best theory of the moon's formation is that 30 to 40 million years after the Earth formed, Earth was hit by a Mars-sized world, throwing huge amounts of the planet's crust and mantle into orbit. After about 100 million years, much of the material from the impact coalesced and cooled to form the moon.

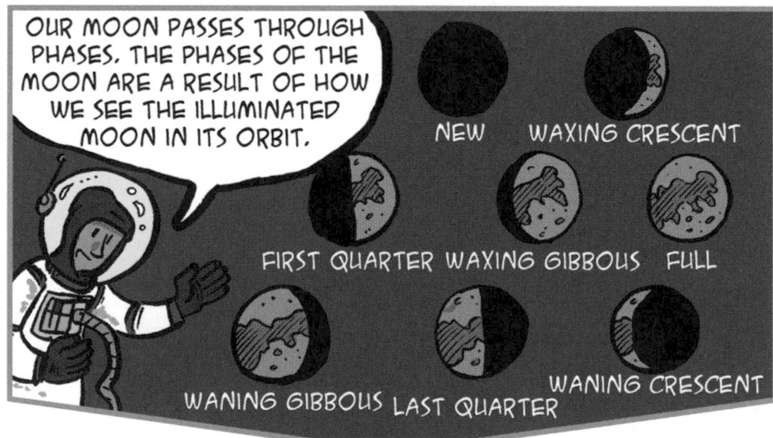

By studying measurements from the lunar surface, scientists deduced that the center of the moon is probably a solid iron core surrounded by a thin layer of liquid iron. Above the core, a mostly hard mantle of rock supports a crust covered in smooth lava plains called mare, and rocky, mountainous, mostly cratered terrain called highlands.

All sizes of craters can be seen from Earth with a simple pair of binoculars. You can also see mountains, volcanic plains, and even extinct volcanoes. With no atmosphere or magnetic field to protect it, the moon was pummeled by asteroids, meteoroids, and comets, leaving behind a pile of rubble atop its crust called regolith. We last visited the moon in 1972. Instead of a return to the lunar surface, many people have their sights set on Mars, the Red Planet.

MARS FACTS

Mars is the most Earth-like planet we know. We've sent flyby missions, landers, rovers, and orbiters to study its climate, geology, history, and potential as a second home for humans. It has towering volcanoes, vast canyons, and icy polar caps. Planet-wide dust storms sometimes hide its surface, and clouds can be seen floating in its thin atmosphere.

While there's evidence that Mars was once a warmer and wetter world more like Earth, today's Mars is cold, dry, and very inhospitable to life—at least on the surface.

About 1.5 times farther from the sun than Earth, the slightly elliptical orbit of Mars takes about 687 Earth days to complete. A diameter of 4,222 miles makes Mars a small world, larger than Mercury but only about half as wide as Earth.

By returning to Earth with rocks from different areas of the moon, the Apollo astronauts helped geologists understand the history of the moon and its evolution.

THE WAR OF THE WORLDS

H.G. Wells's classic novel *The War of the Worlds* features an ancient Martian civilization fleeing its desert world to conquer the Earth. The book was even turned into a radio play that was so well done, people thought it was real! You can find the book at your local library or check out the radio play here.

PS

Orson Welles War Worlds radio

Mars is the least dense of the terrestrial planets, containing only a tenth of Earth's mass. Because of its low mass, on Mars you'd weigh only a third of what you weigh back on Earth.

Although its year is almost twice as long, a day on Mars is a very Earth-like 24 hours and 40 minutes. An axial tilt of 25 degrees gives the Red Planet seasons. With Mars's 687-day year, these seasons last for more than five Earth months each. A very thin atmosphere surrounds the planet, with occasional high clouds and even dust devils twirling their way across a cratered and rocky surface that looks a lot like the driest deserts on Earth.

THE MARTIAN ATMOSPHERE

In the late 1800s, rumors of an ancient civilization on Mars swept around the world. A number of astronomers thought they saw long canals and channels on Mars, built by an alien race to move water around the desert world. But when *Mariner 4* returned the close-up pictures of Mars in 1965, the last hopes of finding the Martians of science fiction were dashed.

Instead of an ancient civilization and its crisscrossing canals, *Mariner 4* sent back pictures of a dry and heavily cratered world. While science fiction fans felt let down by the discovery, planetary scientists were eager to learn more—the exploration of Mars was just beginning.

On Mars, clouds made from crystals of frozen water and carbon dioxide ice occasionally drift through an atmosphere that's made mostly of carbon dioxide and a small amount of nitrogen. At the surface, the atmospheric pressure is just 1 percent of Earth's at sea level. Even though it's thin, the Martian air can still produce winds and massive dust storms that can cover the entire planet for weeks at a time.

With no oceans or seas, Mars has about as much land area as Earth, despite its smaller size!

With its thin atmosphere and greater distance from the sun, the average temperature on Mars is much cooler than Earth—a chilly -51 degrees Fahrenheit (-46 degrees Celsius). But, as on Earth, temperatures can change with the seasons. At the height of Martian summer, temperatures can rise as high as 68 degrees Fahrenheit (20 degrees Celsius)—a nice warm day!

THE SURFACE OF MARS

Dry and dusty, much of Mars's surface resembles some of the driest and most remote deserts on Earth. But the Red Planet also has some of the most dramatic and breathtaking scenery in the solar system.

Ice caps made of water ice and frozen carbon dioxide cover both poles, expanding and contracting with the seasons. At 124 miles wide and 3.7 miles deep, Valles Marineris is the largest system of canyons in the solar system. It stretches more than 2,485 miles along Mars's equator—that's longer than the United States is wide. The canyons are sometimes filled with fog.

The largest of four giant volcanoes, Olympus Mons rises 15 miles above the Martian surface and stretches more than 311 miles across. It's by far the biggest volcano in the solar system, many times larger than Mauna Loa on Earth. Most of Mars's volcanoes are in its Northern Hemisphere, which sits lower and has many fewer craters than the Southern Hemisphere. These volcanoes are either extinct or not currently erupting.

Planetary scientists think that something in the distant past resurfaced or covered the Northern Hemisphere for millions or even billions of years–perhaps a giant sea.

Red Mars

Have you spotted Mars in the sky? It's red coloring is easy to spot from Earth, even without a telescope. Mars's color comes from iron oxide, the same chemical that gives rust its color. So why isn't Earth red? Scientists think that as Earth was cooling slowly, most of its iron sunk beneath the surface. But thanks to its smaller size, Mars cooled too quickly, leaving a lot more iron on the surface to give it its rusty hue.

A Ring Around Mars

Saturn is known for its immense and breathtaking ring system, but Mars might be joining the club in 25 to 75 million years. Planetary scientists studying Mars's innermost moon, Phobos, predict that the tiny satellite will eventually break apart due to tidal forces as its orbit slowly gets closer to the planet. If that happens, the remains of Phobos could form a ring around Mars! The moon already shows signs of the process. Grooves on the face of the potato-shaped moon are thought to be the result of Mars's gravity pulling it apart. Check out this link to learn more!

THE MOONS OF MARS

Mars has two moons. Phobos and Deimos, discovered in 1877, are named after the sons of the Greek war god, Ares. *Phobos* means "fear," and *Deimos* means "terror." These two tiny satellites have diameters of only 6 to 12 miles each and are thought to be asteroids captured from the asteroid belt.

Phobos zips around Mars three times every day at just 3,728 miles above the surface. This makes it the closest moon to a planet in the solar system. Deimos is farther away, and completes an orbit of Mars once every 30 hours.

WATER ON MARS

With such cold temperatures and low atmospheric pressure, lakes and seas can't exist on Mars today. But in the distant past, Mars seems to have been a much warmer and wetter world and the evidence is piling up fast. Detailed images from spacecraft such as NASA's *Mars Reconnaissance Orbiter* and ESA's *Mars Express* show what look like ancient lake beds, rivers, and even ancient coastlines that are billions of years old. Radar and infrared imagining found large amounts of water not just at the poles, but also buried underneath the surface.

In 2004, the *Spirit* and *Opportunity* rovers found rocks on the Martian surface that could be made only in the presence of water. And most recently, the car-sized rover *Curiosity* found layers of ancient sedimentary rock in the remains of an ancient riverbed. All these signs point to a warmer and wetter Mars—so what happened to the water?

Due to the small size of Mars, scientists think that the planet cooled off too quickly, shutting down its magnetic field. Unprotected from cosmic radiation, the atmosphere and much of the water vapor it held was stripped away, cooling the planet and drying out the surface. As the temperatures and pressures dropped, the remaining subsurface water gradually froze, leaving us with the Mars we see today. But if Mars was once warm and wet, could life have gotten a start there as it did on Earth? Could some form of life still exist there today?

LIFE ON THE RED PLANET

On Earth, biologists find life pretty much wherever they look. Forms of bacteria have been found deep within Earth, in the frozen ice sheets of Antarctica, and even in deserts that go without rain for years at a time.

SPACE ELEMENT

The scientists who work with the *Curiosity* rover sometimes have to work odd hours. Because Mars's day is slightly longer than a day on Earth, they follow a Martian time schedule and sometimes have to work late at night—whenever it's daylight on Mars!

This photograph from NASA's *Curiosity* Mars rover shows a pattern typical of a lake-floor sedimentary deposit not far from where flowing water entered a lake.

PS

photo credit: NASA/JPL-CALTECH/MSSS

These organisms, called extremophiles, seem to thrive in places that most of us would find very unwelcoming. Biologists think there's a possibility that organisms similar to extremophiles could find a place on Mars to survive—perhaps deep beneath the soil and away from the deadly radiation on the surface.

The red planet has water and many of the chemicals needed for life to survive, so why haven't we found any? The *Curiosity* rover and the other surface missions weren't designed to look for present life on Mars, but to find out if it was capable of ever supporting life. Now that it looks very possible, the next generation of rovers and landers is being designed with the tools needed to hunt for life on the surface and below.

CURIOUS ABOUT *CURIOSITY?*

Curiosity is a 1-ton mobile chemistry lab on Mars. It contains many instruments to study the rocks and soil of Mars, including a drill, laser, and 17 different cameras. *Curiosity* can also scoop up samples of Martian soil and cook it in a tiny, onboard oven to "sniff" for certain chemicals needed to sustain life. Using all these instruments together, planetary scientists have discovered that Mars was capable of supporting life in the past. To learn more about *Curiosity*, check out this link!

PS

Mars Curiosity NASA

WHAT'S NEXT FOR MARS?

Scientists still have lots of questions about this planet. Does Mars have life today? Can we find evidence of past life? What is the interior of Mars really like? There are a number of upcoming missions designed to answer these questions.

So far, the exploration of Mars has told us a lot about its surface, but very little about what's inside the planet. In fact, we know surprisingly little about how the terrestrial planets formed and what they look like on the inside. A stationary lander called *InSight* has been designed to learn not just about Mars, but also about how all the terrestrial planets formed in the early solar system.

InSight will study the size and composition of the core, mantle, and crust of Mars to learn about its formation. It will carry a seismometer to measure "marsquakes." A 16-foot hole will be drilled and thermometers will go inside the hole to measure temperatures from inside Mars.

In the search for life, both NASA and the ESA have big plans for Mars. Based on *Curiosity*, a new rover called *Mars 2020* will use a lot of the same hardware, but carry new and improved instruments, including cameras capable of taking detailed pictures and movies. Using ground-penetrating radar, the rover will peer beneath the Martian crust to determine its structure and composition. And an experiment called MOXIE will attempt to make oxygen from the carbon dioxide in the atmosphere, which could be used for a future human visit or even as rocket fuel.

Mars 2020 will also house valuable samples for a future mission to collect and return to Earth.

The ESA and Russia are also teaming up to send a rover to the Red Planet in 2020. Called *ExoMars 2020*, this cart-sized laboratory will carry ground-penetrating radar and a 6.5-foot drill to look for organic materials and bio-markers beneath the surface. *ExoMars* will also collect data on temperature, pressure, wind, and moisture. If both missions go well, we might have an answer about life on Mars soon!

KEY QUESTIONS

- **What do we know about Earth and Mars that tells us why one is covered in life while the other seems to be a dead world?**
- **Why do we know more about Earth and Mars than we do about other planets?**
- **Why might we need to colonize another planet?**

VOCAB LAB 

Write down what you think each word means. What root words can you find that will help?

habitable zone, **radiation**, **hydrologic cycle**, **molten**, **erosion**, **ejecta**, **climate change**, **extremophile**, and **bio-marker**.

Compare your definitions with those of your friends or classmates. Did you all come up with the same meanings? Turn to the text and glossary if you need help.

Inquire & Investigate

MODELING THE INNER PLANETS

How do Mercury, Venus, Earth, and Mars compare to each other? We consider these planets as one group, but there are many differences between them. Use models to explore their differences and similarities.

- **Create scale models of the inner planets, being sure to keep the scale the same for each planet.** You can use any material you like—balls, papier mâché, food—whatever you think will work best.
- **If you need help figuring out the right scale for your planets, this website can help.** solar system scale 
- **What can you use to provide detail to your models?** How can you create Mercury's craters or Mars's ice caps?

To investigate more, try modeling Phobos and Deimos, the moons of Mars. How would you model their odd shapes? Based on your scale size, how far apart would each model planet need to be to accurately represent their real-world distances?

INVESTIGATE THE HYDROLOGIC CYCLE

The hydrologic cycle, or water cycle, is an important process on Earth. Water moves between rivers, oceans, the atmosphere, and the land in a continuous system. The hydrologic cycle shapes the land and provides life with its most important resource.

As water moves through the hydrologic cycle, it takes on three states: liquid (water), solid (ice), or gas (water vapor). Energy from the sun drives this cycle. When the sun heats the Earth, some of the water evaporates into the air as water vapor. As it rises into the cooler atmosphere, the water vapor condenses into rain and falls back to Earth to collect in rivers, lakes, oceans, and ice. It then begins the whole process again!

- **How can you create your own examples of water's three states?** Where might you see these states out in the world?
- **Do your own research on the hydrologic cycle, and create a diagram to illustrate what you believe to be the most important parts of the process.** Remember to provide a title, labels, and a legend so others can understand your work!
- **Can you create a model of the hydrologic cycle?** You might need a heat source, something cold, and, of course, some water. How can you measure the changes in your model?

To investigate more, research water on Mars. Is there a hydrologic cycle on Mars, or something like it? Explain your research and your conclusions. How can astronauts recreate a hydrologic cycle while traveling in space or on another planet?

Inquire & Investigate

MODEL THE EARTH-MOON SYSTEM

The Earth-moon system is one we're all familiar with, and it's one of the most unique pairs in the solar system. From any place on Earth, you can watch the moon as it moves through its phases. If you're in the right place at the right time, you just might catch a lunar eclipse! This is when the moon moves so that Earth is in between the sun and the moon. It is different from a solar eclipse, which happens when the moon moves in between the sun and Earth.

On Earth, the moon is visible from pretty much any location. But is the Earth visible from everywhere on the moon?

- **Create a scale model of the Earth-moon system.** Make sure your models are of the correct sizes and distance.
- **Recreate the moon's phases using your scale model.** Where in its orbit do the different phases appear? Create and label a diagram of your results.
- **Create both a lunar and a solar eclipse with your scale model.** Is one more difficult to create than the other?

To investigate more, use your model to describe what Earth would look like from the moon. Would it appear smaller, larger, or the same size as the moon from Earth? If you were on the moon, do you think you'd see the Earth go through phases too? Create and label a diagram with your results.

Chapter 3

The Gas Giants: Jupiter and Saturn

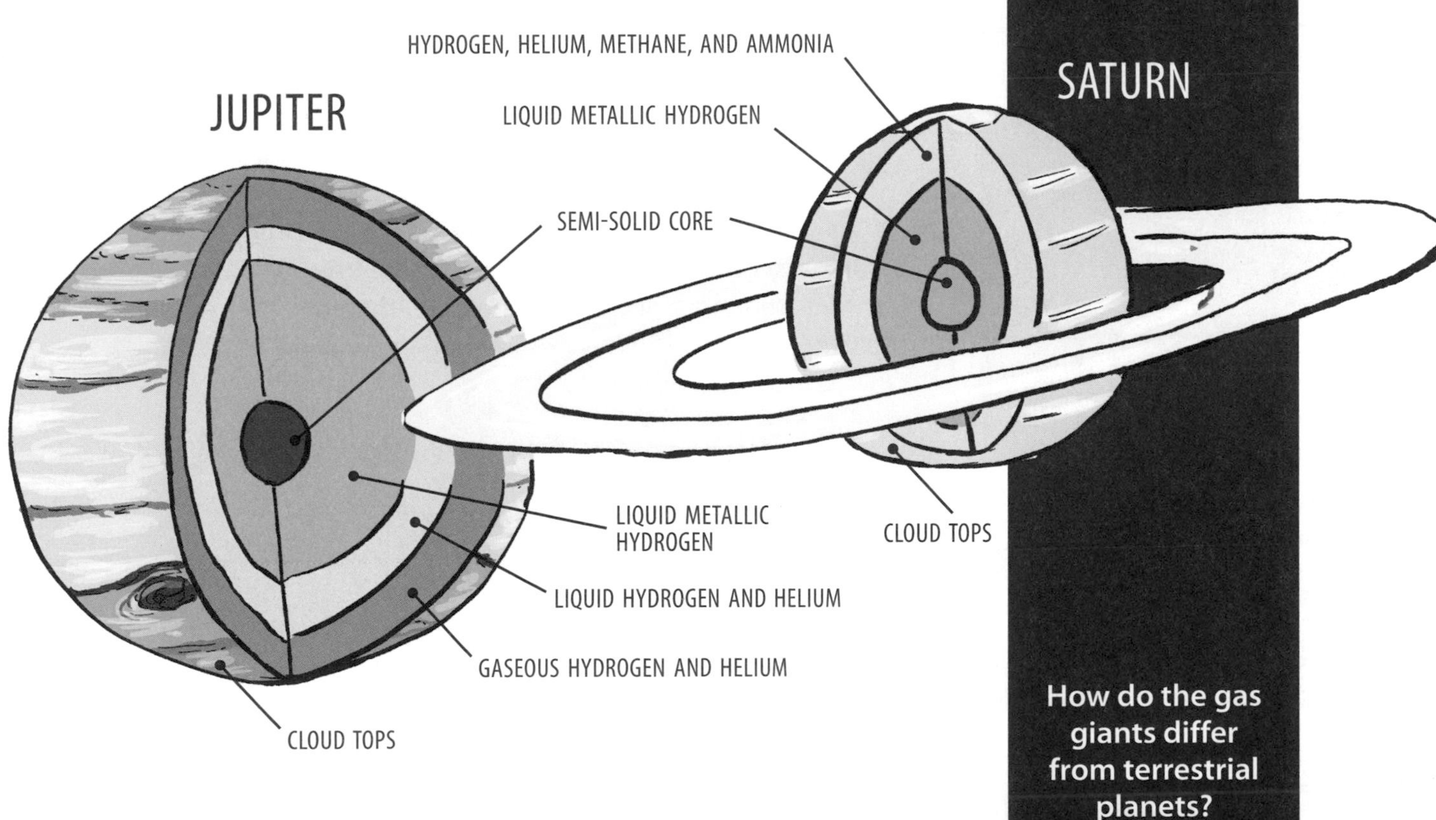

How do the gas giants differ from terrestrial planets?

Planets in the outer solar system have very different atmospheres, surfaces, and internal structures from those found on planets closer to the sun.

Far beyond the terrestrial planets, Jupiter and Saturn rule the solar system. These massive worlds, each many times the size of Earth, feature giant storms, ring systems, and dozens of moons. Some of those moons are even larger than the planet Mercury.

Jupiter and Saturn are two worlds that are very different from the planets of the inner solar system.

As gas giants, the physical structures of Jupiter and Saturn are completely unlike those of the inner planets, having taken most of the solar nebula's material after the sun.

Together, these giants of the solar system fascinated ancient sky watchers and remain important destinations in the solar system for planetary scientists.

JUPITER FACTS

The fifth planet from the sun, Jupiter is home to more than 50 moons. It is wider than 11 Earths and more massive than all the other planets, dwarf planets, asteroids, and comets combined! Storms the size of Earth swirl inside colorful cloud bands that wrap around the entire planet, while four planet-sized moons and dozens of smaller satellites orbit in a miniature version of the solar system.

Since the 1970s, Jupiter has been studied in detail by many space probes, including short flybys by the *Pioneer* and *Voyager* spacecraft and the 8-year-long *Galileo* mission. These visits returned incredible close-up pictures and important data about Jupiter and its moons. Discoveries include its faint ring system, powerful magnetic field, volcanoes on the moon Io, and the possibility of life below the surface of Europa.

Jupiter accounts for 99 percent of all the mass of the solar system that's not the sun.

This planet has a diameter of 88,000 miles and if you could put Jupiter on a scale, it would weigh as much as 318 times Earth's weight. At 483 million miles from the sun, the largest gas giant is more than five times farther from the sun than Earth. It takes Jupiter 11.86 Earth years to complete a single orbit. But the quickly spinning planet's day lasts only 9 hours and 50 minutes—the shortest day of all the planets.

A Failed Star

Jupiter is sometimes called a failed star, but that's not quite accurate. To be a star, an object needs to be massive enough to produce nuclear fusion at its core. Nuclear fusion is the process that causes stars to shine and emit energy. Although it's made mostly of hydrogen and helium, like the sun, Jupiter would need to be about 70 times more massive to start nuclear fusion.

> This rotation is so quick that it affects Jupiter's shape. Instead of nearly being a sphere, Jupiter bulges slightly at its equator.

WHAT SHAPE IS A PLANET?

Although they might look perfectly round in pictures, planets aren't perfect spheres. Things that spin on an axis tend to bulge at the equator and flatten at the poles. This squashed shape is called an oblate spheroid. Because giant planets are made mostly of gases, their bulging equators are easier to see. Terrestrial planets, such as Earth, are squashed, too, but because they're made of denser stuff, they don't squash as easily. On average, Earth is 13 miles wider at the equator than at its poles!

As you might suspect for a such a huge planet, the force of gravity on Jupiter is stronger than it is on Earth. On Jupiter you'd weigh 2.5 times your Earth weight, but you'd have a hard time finding a place to weigh yourself. That's because as a gas giant, Jupiter has no solid surface. Instead, it's made of the same stuff as the sun—mostly hydrogen, a little helium, and just a little bit of other elements.

With an axial tilt of just over 3 degrees and a very circular orbit, Jupiter shows few seasonal changes during its long year. Spots and storms seem to come and go randomly, driven by the hidden interior of this massive world.

EXPLORING JUPITER

What we can see of Jupiter is only skin deep. Colorful clouds of ammonia, ammonium hydrosulfide, and water float in the thin hydrogen atmosphere, zipping around the planet at speeds that can reach 373 miles an hour near the equator. These fast-moving bands travel in opposite directions, and where they meet, powerful storms and eddies churn. Here, a storm wider than Earth called the Great Red Spot has raged for centuries, while dozens of smaller storms and spots come and go.

The beautiful reds, browns, and oranges are thought to be phosphorus and sulfur compounds rising from the planet's warm interior in a process called convection. But the clouds we see represent only a tiny fraction of the giant planet.

This upper-most part of Jupiter is thought to be only 19 miles deep. Beneath the gorgeous storms and colorful bands, planetary scientists suspect some very strange things are happening deep inside the massive world.

On terrestrial planets, the atmosphere simply ends where the ground begins. But for Jupiter and other gas giants, it's not that simple. With no solid surface beneath the clouds, the atmosphere only gets more and more dense. Scientists believe that as the pressure and temperature increase, the hydrogen and helium in the mantle gradually start behaving less like gases and more like fluids, eventually forming an ocean of liquid hydrogen far larger and stranger than anything on Earth.

Deeper still, pressures that are 2 to 3 million times greater than those on Earth squeeze the liquid hydrogen together until it can conduct electricity like a metal. This inner layer of liquid metallic hydrogen, combined with Jupiter's fast rotation, is thought to be responsible for generating the largest magnetic field in the solar system, aside from the sun.

In 1995, the *Galileo* spacecraft dropped a probe into Jupiter's atmosphere. As it plummeted, the probe recorded pressure and temperature readings, giving scientists a firsthand report of Jupiter's upper cloud layers. Just 80 minutes later, the probe stopped transmitting, likely crushed under pressures much higher than it could stand.

Jupiter's Great Red Spot

PS

photo credit: NASA/JPL/Space Science Institute

GALILEO

Without a surface to land on, exploring gas giants such as Jupiter isn't easy. While the *Pioneer* and *Voyager* probes made passing observations of Jupiter and its environment, NASA's *Galileo* orbiter spent nearly eight years studying the Jupiter system in detail. Before plunging to its end in 2003, *Galileo* sent back data on Jupiter's composition, its moons, and faint system of rings, and even dropped a probe into the upper atmosphere. Check out more about the *Galileo* mission here.

NASA Galileo

What's beneath this layer of metallic hydrogen is an even greater mystery. At the center of Jupiter, the pressure and temperature would be unimaginable—maybe 40 million times greater than the pressure at Earth's surface and 63,000 degrees Fahrenheit (35,000 degrees Celsius).

> Here, rock, metals, and other heavy elements might make a core 12,000 miles wide, nearly twice the size of Earth.

Scientists aren't sure if Jupiter's core is solid like the cores of the terrestrial planets or more of a super-dense liquid soup, but precise measurements of the planet's gravity might help reveal what lies at Jupiter's heart.

Jupiter's thin rings were discovered during *Voyager 1*'s flyby in 1979. Jupiter's outer gossamer rings are shepherded by the tiny moons Amalthea and Thebe, while the wider main ring includes Adrastea and Metis. These rings are probably formed from dust and debris from these small moons as they collide with pieces of debris left over from a larger impact.

THE MOONS OF JUPITER

When Italian astronomer Galileo Galilei first pointed his homemade telescope at Jupiter in 1610, he received a bit of a shock. Through his eyepiece, the planet wasn't just a point of light in the sky, it was a brilliant disk surrounded by four small "stars." Galileo quickly discovered that these small "stars" were circling satellites, giving the first direct evidence that not everything in the universe circled Earth.

Ganymede is the largest moon in the solar system. Its diameter of 3,273 miles makes it wider than our moon and even wider than the planet Mercury.

Ganymede's mostly grey surface has a mixture of ancient and heavily cratered areas combined with younger, lighter, grooved regions thought to be formed by water rising from below. These fresher areas tell planetary scientists that Ganymede might have been geologically active in the not-too-distant past, when water flowed onto the surface and erased older, more cratered terrain as it froze.

Scientists think Ganymede's interior is separated into three distinct layers. The moon's crust is a thick, icy shell perhaps 500 miles deep, surrounding a mantle that probably contains a mixture of water and ices. A small iron core at the moon's center would explain the satellite's weak but measurable magnetic field. The planet-sized moon also has a very thin atmosphere of oxygen, but it would be far too thin and cold for us to breath.

If Ganymede orbited the sun instead of Jupiter, it would be a fascinating planet on its own!

GALILEAN SATELLITES

In honor of their discoverer, the four largest moons of Jupiter became known as the Galilean satellites. Today, even the best telescopes on Earth can't see these worlds in much detail. But visits by the *Voyager* probes and the *Galileo* orbiter showed them to be unique and fascinating worlds, changing our understanding of the solar system again.

Because Ganymede is made of a less dense mixture of ice and rock, it's less than half the mass of Mercury.

Callisto, the second largest satellite of Jupiter and only slightly smaller than Mercury, is the most heavily cratered place in the solar system. Thousands of craters overlap on its pockmarked surface, hinting at a surface that hasn't changed much in the 4.6 billion years since it formed.

Unlike on Ganymede, Callisto's surface has none of the lighter groove patterns or smooth plains. Although planetary scientists think that Callisto's interior might be similar to that of its larger sibling, this most distant of the Galilean moons seems to have cooled off quickly after its formation.

PS

Prometheus Plume on Io

photo credit: NASA/JPL

Without heat from its interior, Callisto wouldn't be able to refresh its surface, leaving the craters to pile up on each other.

While Ganymede and Callisto are calm and cratered worlds, Io is something completely different. Io is the most volcanically active object in the solar system. Volcanic vents, geysers, and volcanoes spew molten rock, sulfur dioxide, and other compounds as far as 180 miles into space, much of it falling back to the surface. These eruptions give Io a thin sulfur dioxide atmosphere that would smell like rotten eggs. Lava plains create bright yellows, reds, and oranges that give the moon a pizza-like appearance.

All the activity on the moon's surface is generated by tremendous amounts of gravitational energy from Jupiter. Just as Earth's moon pulls on the oceans to create tides, Jupiter's pull on Io stretches and flexes the entire satellite, causing tides that can lift the surface by as much as 60 miles.

Below Io's colorful crust, these tidal forces keep the rocky mantle molten and supply the surface with enough material to constantly reshape the moon. Scientists think Io has a large liquid iron core at its center.

While Ganymede is the largest, Callisto the most cratered, and Io the most volcanically active, Europa might be the most important moon in the solar system. Bright and icy, Europa's smooth surface is mostly water ice crisscrossed by countless fractures and cracks. Alongside many of these cracks are reddish-brown streaks and stains of an unknown material likely brought to the surface from below. Areas called chaos terrain contain huge chunks of ice that seem to be turning over slowly as warmer material rises beneath the outer crust.

> Europa's young appearance suggests a warm interior, but instead of a mantle of molten rock, Europa may have a giant saltwater ocean beneath its surface.

Since water is the key to life as we understand it, astrobiologists are eager to explore this potentially habitable world. But it won't be easy. Scientists think Europa's icy crust might be 6 to 18 miles thick, which is incredibly thin for a moon that's almost 2,000 miles wide, but still a very long way to drill.

Beneath the crust could be a vast ocean 100 miles deep, with more than twice as much water as all the lakes and oceans of Earth. But at -256 degrees Fahrenheit (-160 degrees Celsius), Europa's surface ice would be as hard as rock on Earth, making it very difficult to penetrate.

EUROPA

There might be another way to get a glimpse of what's happening beneath Europa's icy surface. In 2015, the Hubble telescope recorded what look like plumes of water vapor erupting from Europa. If so, a spacecraft could fly through and sample these plumes to see if the ocean contains the right materials for life. In fact, there's an expedition in the planning stages right now.

PS

Want to learn more about Europa and its potential for life? Check out this video.

Alien Ocean video

WHAT'S NEXT FOR JUPITER

Europa, the smallest of the four giant moons of Jupiter, might have more water than Earth.

Being the largest planet in the solar system, Jupiter naturally holds some big questions that planetary scientists would like to answer.

Does Jupiter have a solid core or is it something more "squishy"? Where exactly does the liquid hydrogen become metallic? And is Europa capable of supporting life in its alleged ocean? There are a few probes that scientists hope can answer these questions.

After a five-year journey, a probe called *Juno* arrived at Jupiter in 2016. *Juno*'s primary mission is to explore and understand how Jupiter became the giant planet it is today. *Juno* carries many tools to uncover Jupiter's secrets. A magnetometer will measure the planet's magnetic field, giving researchers detailed information about the strength of the field.

By precisely tracking its position in space, *Juno* can explore Jupiter's interior. And, of course, *Juno* will send back incredible images! *Juno* is making a number of elliptical orbits that take it over Jupiter's poles, places that no other spacecraft have seen.

NASA's mission to Europa could have two parts, an orbiter and a lander, to examine the moon up close. An onboard thermal imager will hunt for warm spots that could indicate where water and other compounds might be erupting from the surface. A mass spectrometer will sample material that seems to be jetting into space from cracks on the moon's surface.

> The lander would study the surface up close and might determine where the reddish brown stains are coming from.

ESA's *JUICE*, or JUpiter ICy moons Explorer, will make close-up observations of Europa, Ganymede, and Callisto, as well as Jupiter itself. Although it will spend most of its time studying Ganymede, it will also visit Europa to measure the thickness of its outer shell and study its surface composition. Both missions are scheduled to launch within the next decade, and scientists hope they will lead to even more questions about Jupiter and its moons!

SATURN FACTS

With its golden coloring and magnificent system of rings, the sixth planet is sometimes called the "jewel of the solar system." As the farthest planet known to ancient peoples, Saturn marked the outer edge of the solar system for centuries. The great ringed planet has more than 50 known moons, including the solar system's second-largest satellite, Titan.

Saturn has been visited briefly by several space probes since 1980, while the *Cassini* orbiter began circling the planet in 2004. *Cassini* ended its mission with a dramatic dive into Saturn's atmosphere in 2017, but planetary scientists will be studying its data for years to come.

Although Saturn is almost as wide as Jupiter, it contains only a third of Jupiter's mass. This gives Saturn its low density. In fact, it's even less dense than water. That means Saturn would float—if you could find a big enough bathtub!

The sixth planet orbits the sun at an average distance of 889 million miles, almost twice as far as Jupiter and 10 times farther than Earth. At this distance, it takes Saturn 29.5 Earth years to complete a single orbit. The days on Saturn, like the days on Jupiter, are very short, lasting just 10 hours and 40 minutes.

Thanks to this quick rotation, Saturn is also shaped a little like a flattened beach ball. As a gas giant, the ringed world is huge. With a diameter of 74,898 miles, Saturn is almost 10 times as wide as Earth and it's 95 times more massive. But if you could find a place to stand among the cloud tops, you might not feel much heavier than you do at home on Earth. While almost as wide as Jupiter, Saturn is only a third of Jupiter's mass. This gives the planet a gravitational pull just 1.07 times stronger than Earth's.

Unlike Jupiter, an axial tilt of about 27 degrees gives Saturn seasons. Seasons on Saturn seem to affect its weather, often generating giant storms where the atmosphere receives the most direct sunlight. Below its golden bands of clouds, the gas giant is made of the same stuff as Jupiter—mostly hydrogen and helium with a pinch of other elements. Saturn's most famous feature is its system of rings, which circles the planet around its equator like an ornament.

Saturn's Hexagon

At Saturn's north pole, something weird has taken shape. A huge hexagon about 20,000 miles across was first spotted by *Voyager 1* in 1980, and has been photographed in amazing detail more recently by the *Cassini* orbiter. Meteorologists studying the shape think it's the result of a pattern of waves in the atmosphere, and has probably been there for a very long time. However, there's no hexagon at Saturn's south pole, and nobody knows why!

photo credit: NASA/JPL-Caltech/Space Science Institute

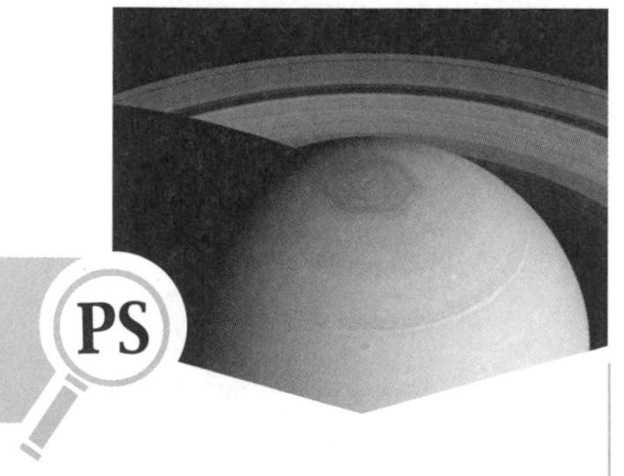

EXPLORING SATURN

The yellow-gold clouds of Saturn are only the very top of its atmosphere. These clouds are made of ammonia, ammonium hydrosulfide, and water ice, just like Jupiter, but the ringed planet's coloration is much different. Planetary scientists aren't sure why this is, but one theory is that Saturn has less material brought to its surface than Jupiter.

The cloud layers are also separated into bands, but they are much harder to see than those on Jupiter. Although Saturn's atmosphere is often quieter and less dazzling than Jupiter's, winds at the equator can move storms and spots at speeds up to 1,118 miles per hour—a dizzying pace. And the ringed planet does have the occasional giant storm.

Known as Great White Spots, these Earth-sized hurricanes can stretch for tens of thousands of miles, and can even circle the entire planet.

Below Saturn's cloud tops, Saturn is thought to be a lot like Jupiter. The hydrogen and helium mantle increases in pressure, density, and temperature until it's crushed into a liquid ocean. Farther down, the fluid turns into liquid metallic hydrogen, conducting electricity and generating a magnetic field 570 times stronger than Earth's, but still much weaker than Jupiter.

Saturn and its rings are easy to view even through a small telescope or binoculars. You can even see the gaps in the rings!

A Great White Spot

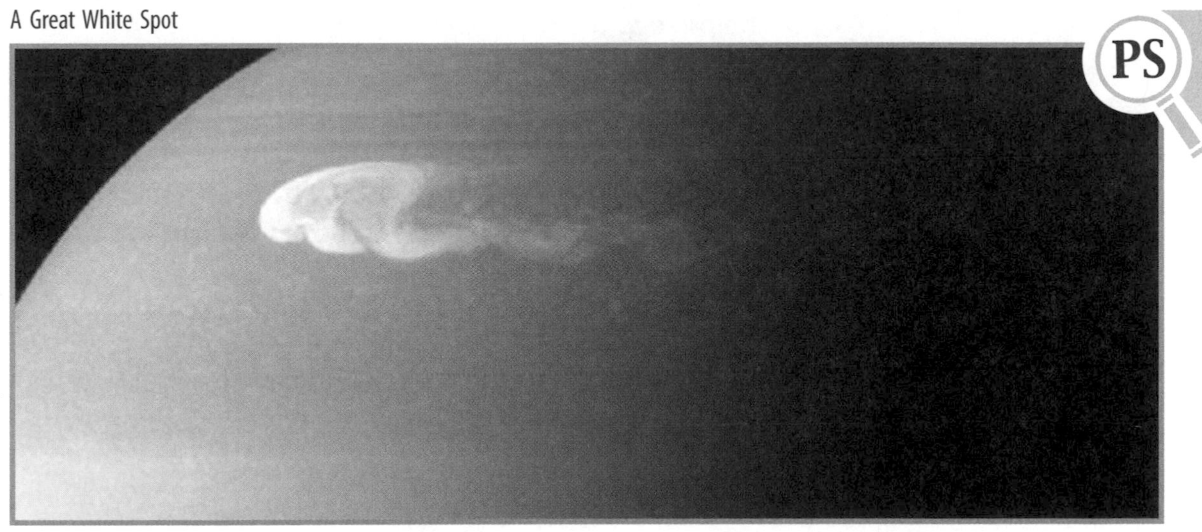

photo credit: NASA/JPL-Caltech/SSI

PS

Although planetary scientists aren't sure if Jupiter has a solid or liquid core, Saturn's lower density makes them more certain that Saturn's core is not solid. With lower pressures and temperatures than Jupiter's interior, Saturn's core is probably a thick soup of metallic hydrogen, rocks, and metals left over from its formation. Thanks to the intense heat and pressure inside Saturn, we're unlikely to ever see the inside of the planet up-close, but at least we can study the planet's most beautiful feature—its rings.

Through *Galileo*'s telescope, the rings we're familiar with looked like two smaller planets on either side of Saturn. In 1659, Dutch astronomer Christiaan Huygens (1629–1695) used a more powerful telescope and was the first to describe what he saw as "rings."

SATURN'S RINGS

Saturn has the largest and most spectacular system of rings in the solar system, easily visible even through a small telescope. The rings are made of billions of particles, ranging in size from grains of dust to chunks of ice to rocks the size of mountains. Spanning more than 173,000 miles in diameter, the rings average between just 10 and 1,000 miles wide—incredibly thin for something so huge. The rings also have gaps that contain fewer particles and look like dark or empty bands. The largest gaps are maintained by Prometheus and Pandora, two oddly shaped "shepherd" moons, whose gravity helps keep the gaps open.

Planetary scientists aren't sure exactly how Saturn's rings formed, but they have some theories.

The rings could be the remains of a small moon that came too close and was torn apart by Saturn's gravity. The bits and chunks of the moon could have spread out to form the ring system we see today.

It's also possible that collisions between comets, asteroids, or other moons helped supply the rings with material. Or maybe they're simply leftover rock and ice from Saturn's formation.

In January 2017, the *Cassini* orbiter began diving through the rings in preparation for its final plunge into Saturn's atmosphere. Scientists hope to sample some of the rings' material and learn about their formation and composition.

Despite the large area they cover, if all the material from Saturn's rings was gathered together, it would create a moon just 62 miles across.

SATURN'S ENIGMATIC MOONS

With 53 known moons and 9 others waiting to be confirmed, Saturn's count of 62 moons is only slightly less than Jupiter's 67. While only massive Titan is the size of the Galilean satellites, Saturn's smaller moons have their own unique quirks. Tiny Prometheus and Pandora orbit within the planet's rings. Another pair, Janus and Epimetheus, orbit so close together that they occasionally swap orbits. And small, grey Mimas has one huge crater that makes it look like the *Death Star* from the science fiction series, *Star Wars*.

SPACE ELEMENT

Saturn's moon Pan is one of the strangest-looking satellites in the solar system. What does it look like to you?

moon or space dumpling?

Saturn's largest moon, Titan, is the second largest in the solar system, and at 3,200 miles across, it's slightly larger than Mercury. From Earth, Titan looks like a pale, fuzzy orange with no surface features. That's because Titan is the only satellite in the solar system with a substantial atmosphere. This thick and hazy envelope of nitrogen and methane hides Titan's surface from view.

In 2004, the *Cassini* orbiter used radar and infrared imaging to peer through Titan's smog and haze for the first time. It also released the *Huygens* probe, a European lander designed to parachute through Titan's atmosphere to its surface. Here's what the mission discovered.

PS

An infrared view of Saturn's moon Titan from NASA's *Cassini* spaceship

photo credit: NASA/JPL/University of Arizona/University of Idaho

Titan's atmosphere extends more than 300 miles above the surface, 10 times higher than Earth's. At the top, sunlight breaks down the methane and nitrogen into carbon compounds, creating Titan's orange smog. Planetary scientists think this strange, soupy mixture is similar to what Earth's atmosphere was like before life began.

At the surface, the pressure on Titan is 1.4 times the Earth's. A visitor there might feel a little as though they were sitting at the bottom of a swimming pool.

But an explorer would still need protection from the frigid temperatures and lack of oxygen. At -288 degrees Fahrenheit (-178 degrees Celsius), Titan's surface is extremely cold. Water ice there is as hard as rock and dunes made of carbon compounds drift like sand. But there are some things that are still liquid even at these temperatures.

On Titan, liquid methane flows like water does on Earth. The super-cold liquid evaporates into the atmosphere and falls to the ground as rain, where it collects in streams and rivers that flow into lakes and even seas. Titan is the only place in the solar system other than Earth to have rivers, lakes, and seas! Using an infrared spectrometer to peer beneath Titan's clouds, *Cassini* captured spectacular views of the frigid seas on the giant moon's surface.

DESCENT TO TITAN

In 2004, the *Huygens* probe detached from *Cassini*, and entered Titan's thick, smog-like atmosphere. During its slow descent to the surface, it captured fantastic images of the hazy world. Check out this video to see Titan up close!

Huygens Titan simulator

Planetary scientists aren't sure where Titan's methane comes from. It's possible that icy cryovolcanoes spew methane and other slushy ices from deep inside the moon, but thanks to the hazy atmosphere, *Cassini* hasn't seen any eruptions. Beneath the crust, Titan could have a mantle of water and ammonia ices surrounding a rocky core. There might even be enough heat inside Titan to form a salty ocean like the one suspected on Jupiter's moon Europa.

On terrestrial worlds, volcanism is the process of molten rock, or magma, flowing from the interior of a planet onto its surface. But with cryovolcanism, water and other ices take the place of rocks and lava. Subsurface water, heated and under pressure, can create geysers, cracks, and even cryovolcanoes that erupt cold, icy lava instead of hot liquid rock!

Although many of the chemicals biologists believe are necessary for life can be found on Titan, it's probably much too cold for life to even get started. But another moon of Saturn might be a more likely place to find living things.

Enceladus, with a diameter of only 313 miles, is much smaller than Titan. But it's not just its size that sets it apart from Saturn's other satellites.

Enceladus looks a lot like Jupiter's moon Europa—its bright, white surface of water ice is crisscrossed by cracks and fractures and has very few craters.

Like Europa, something filled in and resurfaced the moon's ancient landscape, leaving it smoother and brighter than its nearby siblings. But Enceladus's most interesting feature lies beneath its icy surface.

In 2005, the *Cassini* probe detected water vapor erupting from cracks in the surface near the south pole. These cracks, or fissures, were nicknamed tiger stripes and are surrounded by smooth terrain that seems to be very fresh. After sending *Cassini* through these plumes, scientists found that they contain water ice, salts, grains of rock, and carbon compounds. They estimate a sea about 6 miles deep lies underneath 22 miles of ice near Enceladus's south pole.

Just like on Europa, the presence of liquid water makes Enceladus an important place to look for life elsewhere in the solar system.

WHAT'S NEXT ON SATURN

The *Cassini* spacecraft detected organic molecules in Enceladus's icy plumes, but the instruments weren't sensitive enough to determine if they were formed by biological or geochemical processes. Scientists have proposed a mission to take a number of deep "sniffs" of the material erupting from Enceladus's suspected ocean to find out if it is or was an environment capable of supporting life.

For Titan, planetary scientists want to know more about organic compounds found there and more about the suspected hidden saltwater ocean.

Several missions have been proposed to explore Saturn and its moons in more detail, including submarines, balloons, orbiters, and rovers. But these are years away from being built. It might be a long time before we visit Saturn again.

KEY QUESTIONS

- **Why is it so rare to find all the elements needed for life as we know it in the right forms? What does this say about life on Earth?**
- **How do scientists face the challenges of studying planets we can't land on?**

VOCAB LAB 

Write down what you think each word means. What root words can you find that will help?

oblate spheroid, **eddies**, **convection**, **geyser**, **chaos terrain**, **magnetometer**, and **cryovolcanoes**.

Compare your definitions with those of your friends or classmates. Did you all come up with the same meanings? Turn to the text and glossary if you need help.

Inquire & Investigate

SATURN'S RINGS

One of the most awe-inspiring sights in the solar system is Saturn's massive system of rings. Their incredible thinness is hard to imagine, but we can try! Measured from the inside edge to the outside edge, Saturn's rings are about 35,400 miles wide, but only between 33 and 3,000 feet thick.

- **The average sheet of paper is just 0.1 millimeters thick.** If you were to build a scale model of Saturn's rings using paper, how big would the model be?
- **Can you think of anything you could use in a scale model of Saturn that would accurately represent the thickness of the rings?** Why or why not?
- **If you gathered up all of the material in Saturn's rings, it would make a moon only 62 miles across.** What does that say about the density of the rings?

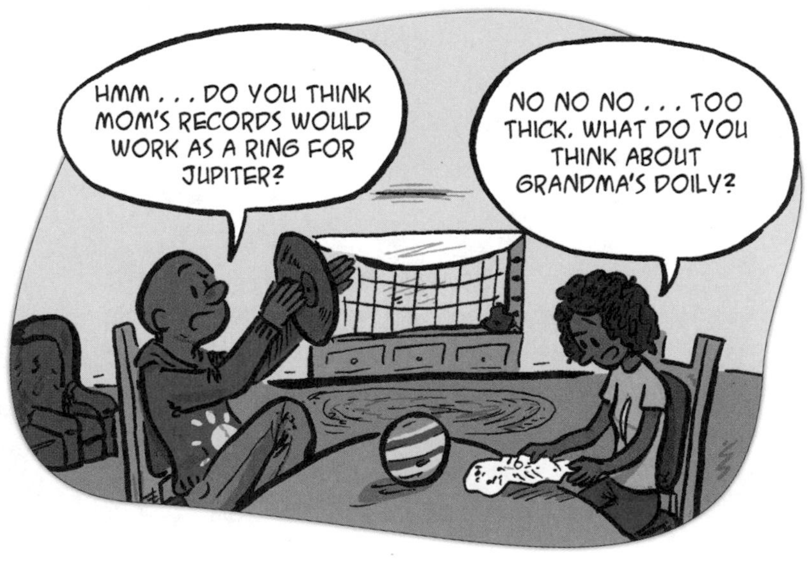

To investigate more, think about how Saturn's rings aren't really one thin sheet, but are made of millions and millions of objects of different sizes. How might you model this?

INVESTIGATE TIDAL FORCES

Both Io and Europa feel the heat from Jupiter's gravitational squeeze, but Io has it the worst. Can you really heat something up by flexing it?

- **You'll need a flexible object—foam rubber balls work best.** If you can, cut holes in the ball just enough to fit a thermometer.
- **Record the starting temperature of the ball as accurately as you can.** Now squeeze! Squeeze and flex the ball for a set amount of time.
- **Record the temperature of the ball you squeezed, and compare it to its starting temperature.** Consider these questions.
    - How much of an increase in temperature did you measure?
    - Are there other ways the ball could have increased in temperature with squeezing or flexing?
    - Trying squeezing the ball for different periods of time. How does it affect the temperature?
    - Why do you think the flexing of an object creates heat?

To investigate more, test how long it takes for the ball to return to its starting temperature. What do you think would happen to the ball if you could keep on squeezing it for hours or days? Would it take longer to cool off?

SPACE ELEMENT

Besides flexing it's grip on moons, Jupiter's gravity can be used for other things—such as exploring the solar system. A number of space probes have used the giant planet's gravity to boost their speed and change direction. It's sometimes called a "gravitational slingshot!"

SPACE ELEMENT

Planetary scientists are undecided about which moon is best suited to look for possible life—Europa or Enceladus. What do you think?

INSIDE EUROPA

With an icy shell, a mantle of saltwater, and a rocky core, Europa is one of the best places for astrobiologists to search for life. But getting to Europa and going below the surface aren't going to be easy.

- **Imagine you are an engineer working for NASA.** You've been called upon to design a Europa explorer mission. Consider these questions.
  - What are your science goals?
  - Do you want a lander, an orbiter, or both?
  - What would your probe's tools include?
  - If you land on Europa, how would you get beneath the surface? What do you think you'd find there?
  - What would you do when you get to the ocean?
- **Put your mission together as a proposal and present it to your friends, family, or class.** What kinds of questions did they ask? Did they have any suggestions?

To investigate more, think about what other satellites of Jupiter you would explore and why. What would it take to explore the other places? For example, how would a craft built to explore Europa differ from one built to explore Io?

Chapter 4

The Ice Giants: Uranus and Neptune

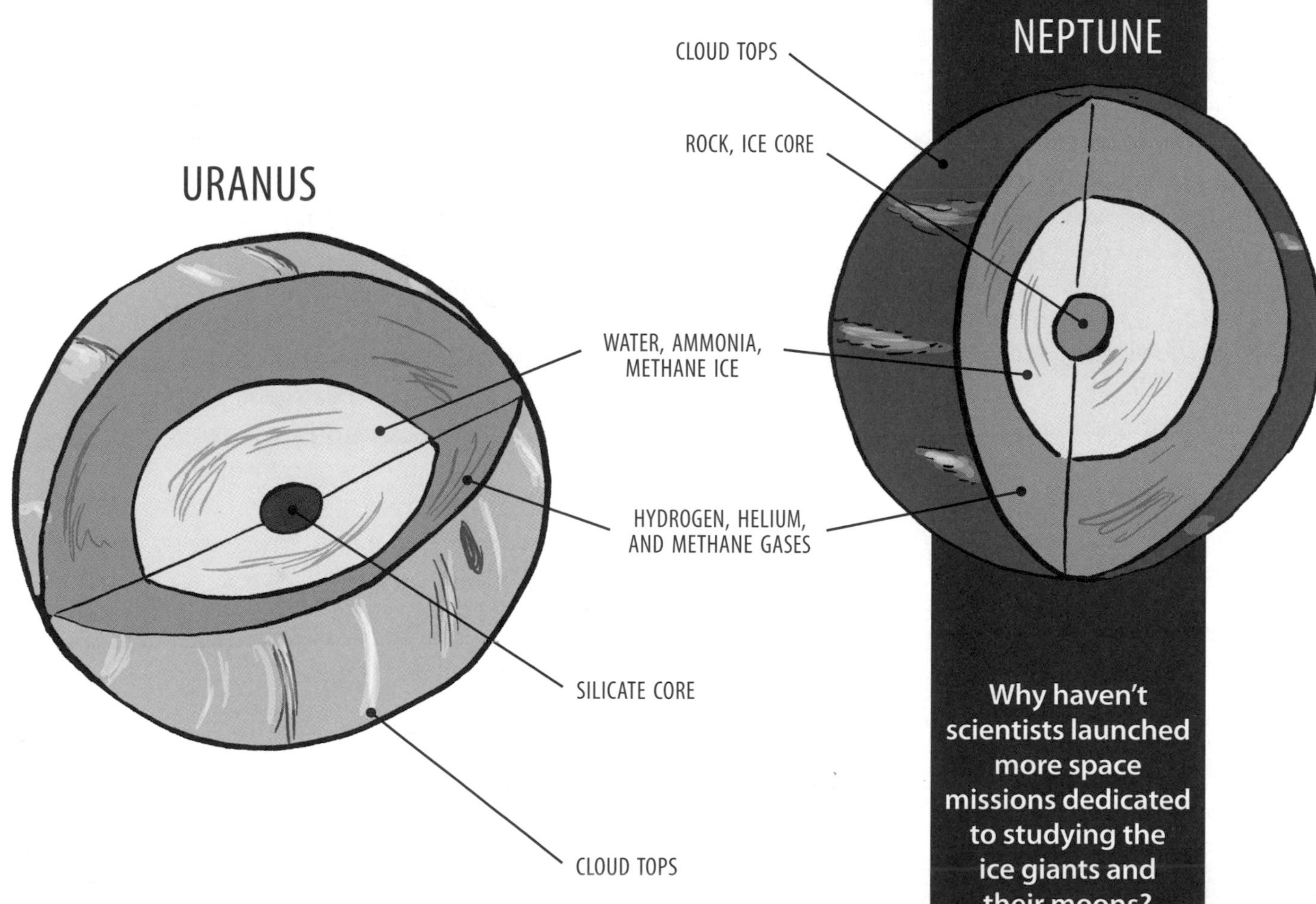

Why haven't scientists launched more space missions dedicated to studying the ice giants and their moons?

It takes a lot of time and money to send spacecraft this far out in the solar system, and only one mission has been planned and executed to date. Maybe more missions will be planned in the future!

Beyond Jupiter and Saturn lie the final two planets in the solar system—Uranus and Neptune. Smaller than the gas giants but still much larger than Earth, these ice giants are cold and distant worlds that were unknown until the invention of the telescope. Like the other giant planets, both Uranus and Neptune have moons and ring systems, but they have their own unique attributes as well.

Uranus, knocked on its side long ago, spends decades with its poles pointing almost directly toward and away from the sun. Neptune is circled backward by its giant moon, Triton, which may be a captured world from much farther out in the solar system. Visited only once, these planets have been watched from a distance while scientists wait for the opportunity to visit them again.

URANUS FACTS

For centuries, Saturn was the furthest planet known to astronomers. But in 1781, the astronomer William Herschel (1738–1822) expanded our view of the solar system when he discovered a faint, blue-green disk with his telescope. His discovery created quite a stir—it was the first planet found that was not known to ancient civilizations.

With Uranus about twice as far from the sun as Saturn, Herschel's sighting of Uranus immediately doubled the size of the solar system and inspired others to look for planets even more faint and distant. A blue-green world with frigid clouds and dark, dusty rings, Uranus remains mysterious and difficult to understand.

A captured world is a general term for a body that orbits a planet, moon, or other object that didn't originally form with or from the thing that it orbits. Mars's moons Phobos and Deimos are thought to be asteroids that formed elsewhere in the solar system but were captured by the planet's gravity. Earth's moon, however, is not a captured world. It formed from a collision between Earth and a Mars-sized planet early in the solar system's formation.

Image of Uranus from *Voyager 2*, 1986

photo credit: NASA/JPL-Caltech

At 31,763 miles across and with a mass 14.5 times more than Earth's, Uranus is larger than the inner planets but smaller than Jupiter and Saturn. Uranus is 19 times farther from the sun than Earth at 1.7 million miles, and receives just a fraction of the sunlight that we do.

As you might guess, this makes Uranus a very cold place. Temperatures at the ice giant's cloud tops measure a frosty -364 degrees Fahrenheit (-220 degrees Celsius), making it the coldest planet in the solar system, colder even than the more distance Neptune.

Uranus completes one rotation in a little more than 17 hours, but sunrise and sunset would look nothing like they do on Earth, because of Uranus's wildly tipped axis. Tilted at 97 degrees, both its north and south poles spend half of the planet's 84-year orbit in sunlight and half in darkness.

Uranus might not have always been tipped over. Planetary scientists think that at some point in Uranus's history, it was clobbered by a massive object that caused it to tip over, similar to how they think Venus ended up "upside down." This tremendous impact might have also been the cause of Uranus's strange, off-center magnetic field.

EXPLORING URANUS

Like Jupiter and Saturn, there's no solid surface on Uranus. Clouds made of ammonia, water, and methane float in a mostly hydrogen and helium upper atmosphere that is the coldest in the solar system. Below the cloud layers, methane gives Uranus its unique color by absorbing red light and reflecting the bluish-green we see in images.

Although the planet looks featureless in many pictures, infrared imaging shows that the atmosphere certainly isn't quiet. Near the equator, bands of clouds race around the planet in opposite directions up to 560 miles (901 kilometers) per hour. During its brief flyby in 1986, *Voyager 2* spotted large storms similar to the massive hurricanes of the gas giants. More recently, different spots and storms appear in images from the Hubble telescope, suggesting Uranus has a very dynamic atmosphere.

Farther in, Uranus is even less understood than Jupiter and Saturn. Like the large worlds, pressures and temperatures likely increase gradually until the gases become more like a fluid. But instead of liquid hydrogen and helium, Uranus's mantle is probably saltwater mixed with methane and ammonia ices, all crushed together under immense pressure.

At an estimated 13,000 degrees Fahrenheit (7,000 degrees Celsius), Uranus's core is cooler than that of the giant planets. With lower temperature and pressures, the center of Uranus is probably a slushy mixture of silicates, rocks, and highly compressed ices.

Although Uranus has no layer of liquid metallic hydrogen, planetary scientists think that Uranus's magnetic field comes from the rotation of its saltwater mantle. Salty water conducts electricity, but not nearly as well as liquid metallic hydrogen. As a result, Uranus's magnetic field is much weaker than its gas giant neighbors, but still 50 times stronger than Earth's. Strangely, Uranus's magnetic field isn't centered on the core, but instead seems to sit off-center in the mantle. This bizarre magnetic field also doesn't line up with the planet's axis. Instead, it's tilted at almost 60 degrees.

Scientists aren't sure why Uranus is so cold, but it might be from the same collision that tipped the planet over. Some planetary scientists think that a large impact removed a piece of Uranus's core, taking its heat with it.

THE RINGS OF URANUS

In 1977, astronomers hoping to study the atmosphere of Uranus watched as the planet occulted, or passed in front of, a distant star. To their surprise, the star seemed to dim before and after it disappeared behind the planet, leading them to believe they'd found evidence for a faint set of rings. In 1986, *Voyager 2* confirmed these observations. Today, there are 13 rings known to circle the ice giant. Uranus's rings are narrower and darker than those of Saturn, with most rings less than 60 miles wide and separated by large empty gaps.

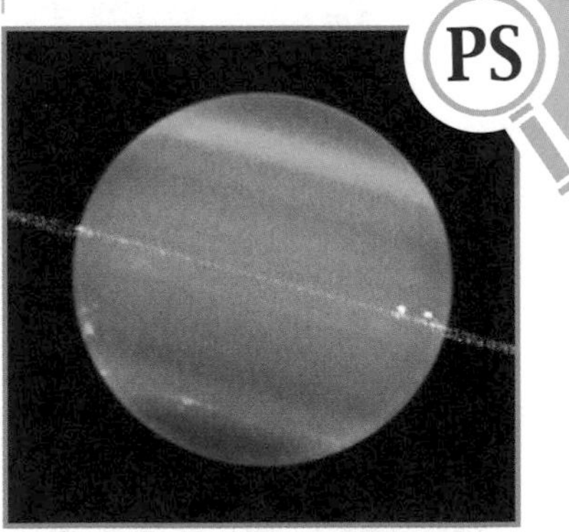

photo credit: W. M. Keck Observatory (Marcos van Dam)

While Saturn's rings are made mostly of bright and reflective ices, Uranus's rings are made of much darker stuff. Planetary scientists think they're coated in carbon compounds, turned dark through exposure to intense solar radiation. This makes them much less reflective and harder to see, especially compared to Saturn's majestic system.

SPACE ELEMENT

Uranus's family of satellites are named after characters from the plays of William Shakespeare and Alexander Pope.

THE MOONS OF URANUS

The inner moons of Uranus are very different from those of Jupiter and Saturn. Like the planet's rings, they appear to be much darker than the mostly icy moons of the gas giants, consisting of an even mixture of rock and ices. They're also smaller. Of the 27 known satellites, there are no giant moons like Jupiter's Ganymede or Saturn's Titan. Four of Uranus's moons have diameters between 600 and 1,000 miles, and the rest are 300 miles across or smaller.

The smallest and most recently discovered moons are the hardest to see. Less than 12 miles across, these are probably captured asteroids and have surfaces darker than asphalt. While not as dazzling as Titan or Europa, Uranus's satellites are still fascinating.

PS

Montage of large Uranian moons

photo credit: NASA

Uranus's two largest moons, Titania and Oberon, were both discovered by William Herschel in 1787. The two moons are similar in size at about 900 miles across. Little is known about them, but both appear to be made of about equal mixtures of ice and rock. Titania's surface is less cratered than Oberon's, which could mean its surface is younger. Giant canyons stretch across much of Titania's surface, hinting at fractures in the crust at some point in its history.

With many more craters, Oberon, a slightly darker moon than Titania, shows less signs of geological activity on its surface. Oberon likely hasn't changed much since it formed.

When a moon has a nickname such as "Frankenstein-moon," you know it's going to be interesting. Even though Miranda is just 292 miles wide, it's not just another small satellite. The images of Miranda from *Voyager 2* show a bizarre and misshapen world, barely massive enough to maintain its shape. Its collection of strange and diverse surface features gives it the appearance of being pieced together from other moons, with young and bright surface features fitted next to ancient cratered plains.

> Planetary scientists aren't sure how Miranda came to be this way.

Miranda also has the largest cliff in the solar system, called Verona Rupes. A more than 6-mile drop makes it five times deeper than the Grand Canyon. A rock dropped from the cliff would take more than eight minutes to hit the bottom, thanks to Miranda's weak gravity.

Liquid Oceans?

It's possible that, like other icy satellites in the solar system, Titania and Oberon have liquid oceans deep below the surface. But the few close-up pictures taken by *Voyager 2* don't show much recent resurfacing.

Voyager 2 Miranda composite

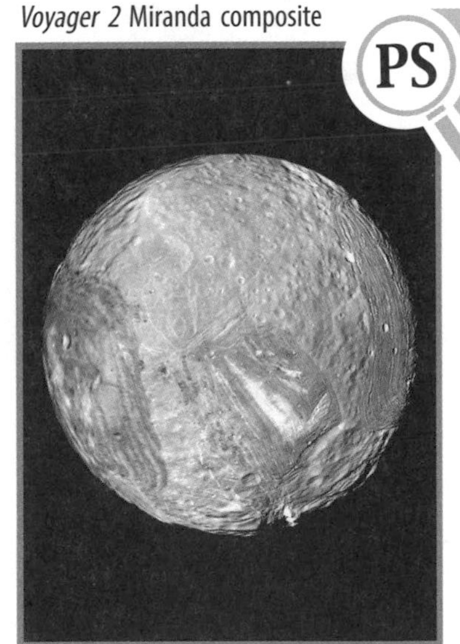

photo credit: NASA/JPL-Caltech

WHAT'S NEXT FOR URANUS

With its seemingly stitched-together surface of odd shapes and terrains, Miranda is a puzzle. How was it formed, and what led to such a bizarre appearance?

Uranus and its moons are some of the least-understood objects in the solar system. After *Voyager 2*'s 1986 encounter, no other space probes have visited Uranus, and there are still lots of questions to be answered about the blue-green world.

One of the biggest questions about Uranus is how it got its crazy axial tilt. Planetary scientists think it was probably knocked over in a huge collision with an Earth-sized object, but it's a hard theory to test. This theory might also explain why Uranus is so cold—if a large part of the planet's interior was lost, a lot of heat might have gone with it. The off-center magnetic field could have something to do with an early impact, too, but some researchers propose that a layer of liquid diamond in Uranus's core might be pushing the field in a certain direction.

Using telescopes on the ground and in space, scientists continue to learn more about the uniquely tilted planetary system, but a dedicated mission is needed to really examine the world and its moons up close. Several have been proposed by planetary scientists around the world, but so far, none have received funding.

Image of Neptune from *Voyager 2*, 1989

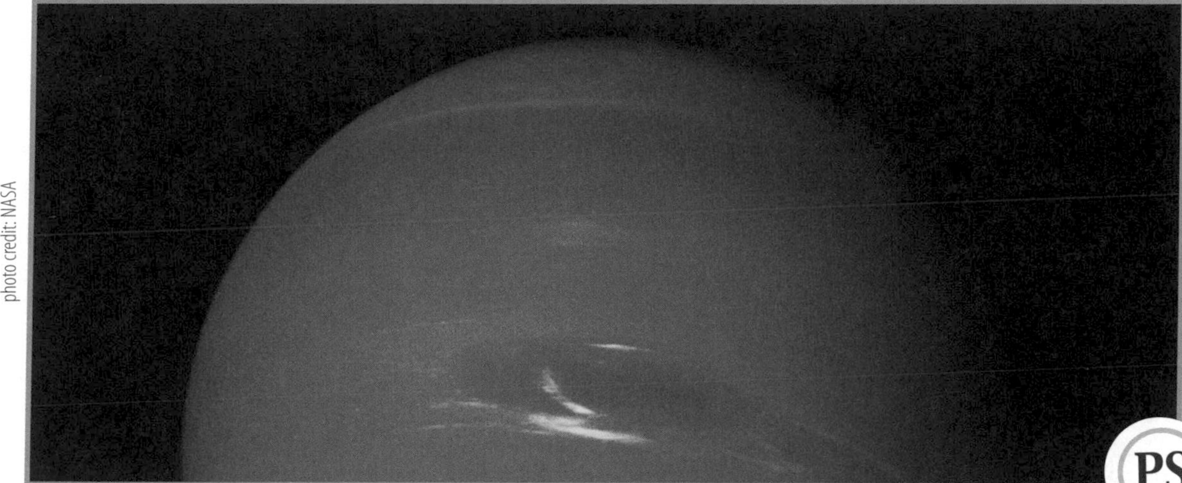

photo credit: NASA

NEPTUNE FACTS

Neptune was found by mathematics before it was seen through a telescope. After the discovery of Uranus, astronomers noticed that the planet's orbit didn't quite match their predictions.

This started a hunt for a new planet, one massive enough to affect Uranus, even at a great distance. Between 1845 and 1846, two astronomers independently predicted the size and location of Neptune, and the planet was finally spotted months later by German astronomer Johann Gottfried Galle (1812–1910). He found it very close to its predicted position.

With Neptune being the farthest planet from the sun, you might expect it to be a cold, quiet world. But the deep-blue planet is anything but a boring place. Although it's made mostly of the same stuff as Uranus, Neptune is a warmer and more active planet. Home to one large moon and many smaller satellites, the most distant planet features storms, an odd set of rings, and the fastest winds in the solar system.

Neptune was named after the Roman god of the sea. It's a fitting name for a vibrantly blue world.

Who Saw Neptune First?

While Neptune was officially discovered in 1846, it was probably seen much earlier. When Galileo Galilei was observing Saturn in 1610, he noted a faint, bluish disc in the background and described it in his journal. By studying the planet's orbits in detail, astronomers could turn back the clock and discover that Neptune was indeed right where Galileo described the faint blue disk. If Galileo had observed it more closely, it's possible Neptune might have been discovered much earlier, even before Uranus.

The eighth and most distant planet, Neptune is 2.7 million miles (4.3 million kilometers) from the sun. At this distance, it takes more than four hours for sunlight to reach the planet's cloud tops. Since its discovery, astronomers have seen Neptune complete just one 165-year-long orbit, the longest period in the solar system. Its diameter of 30,778 miles (49,532 kilometers) makes it a little smaller than Uranus, but despite its lesser size, it's a more massive world, equal to the mass of 17 Earths.

A Neptunian day is 16 hours and 7 minutes long, and its axial tilt of 29 degrees gives it seasons that last for more than 40 years. Neptune is surrounded by 14 moons, including Triton, by far the largest satellite of the ice giants.

Neptune is also circled by an extremely faint and "lumpy" ring system, one that is unique in the solar system.

EXPLORING NEPTUNE: A BLUE AND WINDY WORLD

Although the deep blue of Neptune might look like a solid surface, as on the other giant planets, there's no place to stand. From the top of its clouds to its core, Neptune is much like its neighbor, Uranus. It's atmosphere is made mostly of hydrogen, helium, and methane supporting clouds of ammonia, ammonia hydrosulfide, and water ice. Both *Voyager 2* and the Hubble telescope have measured these clouds moving at speeds around 746 miles (1,200 kilometers) an hour at the equator—the fastest winds in the solar system.

As on Uranus, methane gives Neptune its blue color, but nobody is sure why Neptune is a much deeper shade of blue.

Neptune also has an active atmosphere. During its short flyby in 1989, *Voyager 2* took pictures of a shadowy storm on Neptune called the Great Dark Spot. Half the size of Jupiter's Great Red Spot, this storm seemed to create a window through the upper atmosphere, showing the deeper and darker methane layers below. The Great Dark Spot eventually disappeared, but others like it have crossed Neptune's face during the past few decades.

Neptune's 165-year orbit means it moves very slowly on its path through the sky.

INSIDE NEPTUNE

The interior pressure and temperature of Neptune rise steadily until they become liquid, forming a planet-wide ocean. Neptune probably isn't massive enough to create liquid hydrogen, so the oceanic mantle is thought to be mostly saltwater mixed with ammonia and methane. Because Neptune is a little denser than Uranus, it might have a slightly larger core, possibly the size of Earth's. It would probably be made of iron, nickel, rock, and other heavy elements gathered when the planet first formed.

Without liquid metallic hydrogen, Neptune's magnetic field is likely generated in the salty ocean as the planet spins on its axis. While its magnetic field is only half as strong as Uranus's, they are very similar. Neptune's magnetic field is tipped at 47 degrees from its axis and, like Uranus's, it appears to be centered in the mantle and not the core. Planetary scientists are not sure why.

Neptune clouds

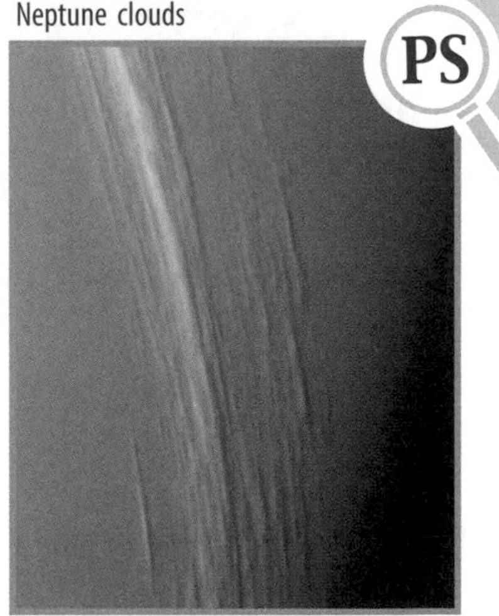

photo credit: NASA/JPL

A GRAND TOUR

In the 1960s, planetary scientists realized they had a golden opportunity to explore the outer solar system. If they launched a probe at just the right time, they could use each planet's gravity to push it on to the next. *Voyager 1*, launched on September 5, 1977, used this special alignment to visit Jupiter and Saturn. But *Voyager 2*, launched on August 20, 1977 (yes, they launched in reverse order!), visited all four of the giant planets, a grand tour indeed! To learn more about the *Voyager* probes and what they're up to today, check out this link!

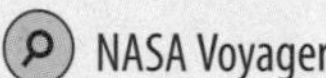

NASA Voyager

NEPTUNE'S STRANGE RINGS

The discovery of Uranus's ring system started a hunt for rings around the other giant planets, including Neptune. Hints of an extremely faint and puzzling set were noticed in the mid-1960s, but weren't confirmed until *Voyager 2*'s visit in 1989. Today, six rings are known to circle Neptune, and they resemble those of Uranus in a few ways. Like Uranus's, Neptune's rings are mostly made of dust and small rocks, probably coated in carbon compounds turned dark by radiation. These indistinct rings also have large gaps between them, making them hard to spot. What really sets Neptune's rings apart is their lumpiness.

Even though it's only 22 miles wide, Neptune's Adams ring is the planet's most interesting. The Adams ring has five distinct ring arcs where material gathers in strange clumps. These arcs are brighter and wider than the rest of the ring system, and were the first hints that some kind of ring orbited the planet.

Planetary scientists still have no good way to explain what created these lumpy sections. They could be due to the gravitational influence of shepherd moons within the rings or even the remains of a recent collision.

THE MOONS OF NEPTUNE

Like the other giant planets, Neptune is home to a number of satellites that come in many sizes and shapes. Of the 14 known moons, most are very small and dark.

Only Nereid and Triton, the two brightest moons, were known when *Voyager 2* first approached the eighth planet. During its short visit, *Voyager 2* found six small moons, and another six were discovered later with the Hubble telescope.

More than half of Neptune's family of satellites are smaller than 60 miles across. At 1,700 miles wide, Triton is by far the largest of the siblings. However, Triton might not be related to the other moons at all.

As the seventh largest moon in the solar system and the largest satellite of the ice giants, Triton dominates the space around Neptune. With a mass nearly twice that of all Neptune's moons and rings combined, Triton stands out not just for its size, but for its highly inclined and retrograde orbit. While all other major moons orbit in the same direction as their planet's rotation, Triton swings around Neptune in the opposite direction.

To planetary scientists, this strange orbit suggests that Triton isn't really a part of Neptune's family and is instead an object that formed farther out in the solar system. It has a lot in common with the dwarf planet Pluto, which suggests they might have formed in the same region of the solar system.

In this image from *Voyager 2*, the dimpled terrain near Triton's south pole gives it the look of a cantaloupe!

PS

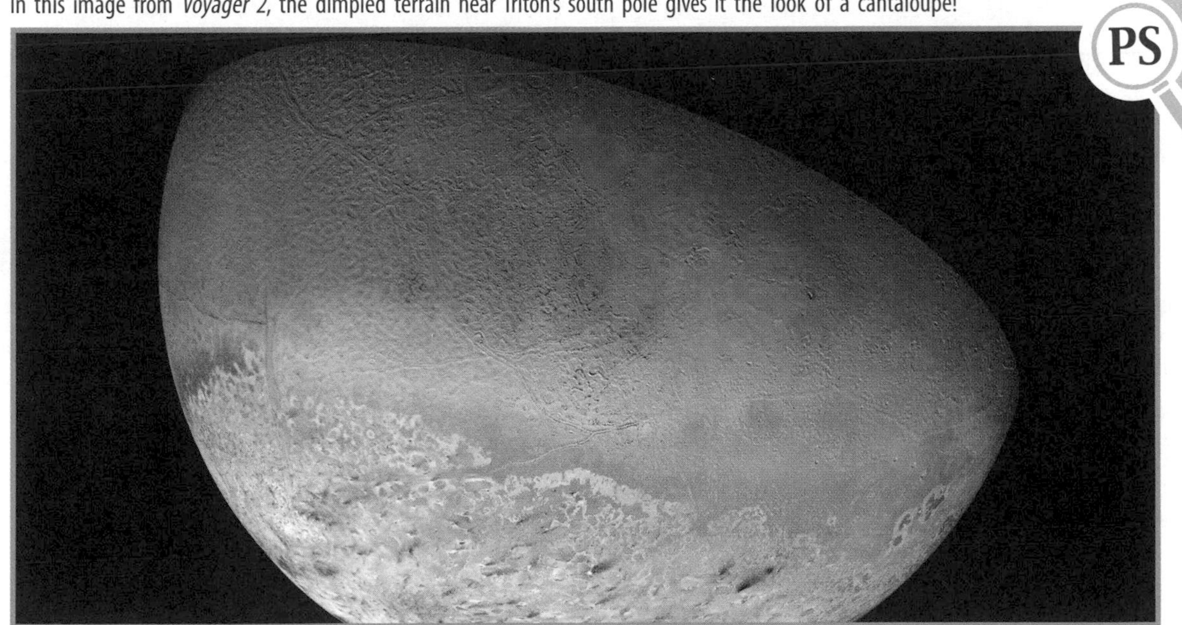

photo credit: NASA/JPL/USGS

The surface of Triton is a mixture of nitrogen, water, and carbon dioxide ices over a mantle that's thought to be made of water ice. When *Voyager 2* approached Neptune and Triton, most scientists expected to see a cold and quiet world covered with ancient craters. Nearly everyone was surprised when *Voyager 2*'s camera captured geysers erupting from the surface of the frozen moon. Like Europa's, the surface of Triton has very few craters and it could be less than 100 million years old—a very young age for the solar system.

Like other large and icy satellites, Triton might have a salty ocean beneath its crust, but a closer look is needed to tell for sure. Radioactivity in its rocky core might provide Triton with enough heat to keep some of the water in a liquid state, powering the geysers and cryovolcanoes on the surface.

Unfortunately for Triton, its backward orbit means the moon is likely doomed to destruction. This pattern is slowly bringing Triton closer to the planet, and in about 3.6 billion years, Neptune's gravity will likely tear the captured moon apart. On the bright side, it might create a spectacular new set of rings that could challenge Saturn for the title, "jewel of the solar system."

VOCAB LAB 

Write down what you think each word means. What root words can you find that will help?

captured world, **dynamic**, **silicate**, **occulted**, **predict**, **retrograde**, **dominate**, and **inclined**.

Compare your definitions with those of your friends or classmates. Did you all come up with the same meanings? Turn to the text and glossary if you need help.

WHAT'S NEXT FOR NEPTUNE?

So far, only *Voyager 2* has visited Neptune and Triton, leaving planetary scientists with a lot of questions. Why is Neptune warmer than Uranus? Where do the rings come from? Is Triton a captured world? A mission named *Argo* was proposed to explore the ice giants and their moons, but was never developed. To really understand the Neptunian system, a large orbiter like *Cassini* is needed, but there aren't any in the planning stages. Ideally, a new mission is chosen soon to explore this windy world and its backward moon.

KEY QUESTIONS

- **Why is it so difficult to send missions to the ice planets?**
- **What might data from these planets tell us about the solar system as a whole?**

Inquire & Investigate

A MISSION TO THE ICE GIANTS

The two ice giants have a lot in common: They're nearly the same size, made of mostly the same stuff, and are circled by their sets of moons and rings. Planetary scientists would love the chance to send a dedicated spacecraft to investigate each in greater detail, but missions to the outer planets are very expensive.

- **Imagine yourself as the principal investigator.** You've been chosen to design and build a space probe capable of exploring these poorly understood worlds. But there's a catch—you can visit only one!
- **While making your decision, think about the following:**
  - What questions need to be answered about each planet? Which do you think are the most important or interesting, and why?
  - What kind of science do you want your mission to accomplish? Is it an orbiter, a lander, or something else?
- **When missions are chosen, they're often judged by more than just the amount of knowledge they can gain about the planet they visit.** Missions are chosen by how they might help us understand the solar system as a whole. Think about what studying each planet can teach us about the solar system.
- **Compose an argument to defend your planet of choice.** Your argument can be made in any form you like—a presentation, a written paper, charts or diagrams—it's your choice!

To investigate more, have a friend, classmate, or family member choose their preferred planet and have a debate. What reasons can you give to defend your choice? Take the other side and try arguing for the planet you didn't choose. Does it change your mind? Why or why not?

Inquire & Investigate

MODELING THE OUTER PLANETS

How do the sizes and features of the giant planets compare to each other and to the planets of the inner solar system?

- **Create scale models of the giant planets.** As with the terrestrial planets, you can use any materials you like, as long as the scale is consistent.
- **If you're having trouble finding a good scale size for your planets, check out this website for some guidance.**  build solar system 
- **What can you use to provide detail to your models?** How can you create Saturn's rings or Jupiter's brightly colored clouds?

To investigate more, create models of the giant moons. What should their distances be from their model planets? Can you build an entire solar system to scale? How large would your model of the sun be? How large would your model solar system be?

Chapter 5

Dwarf Planets, Asteroids, and Comets

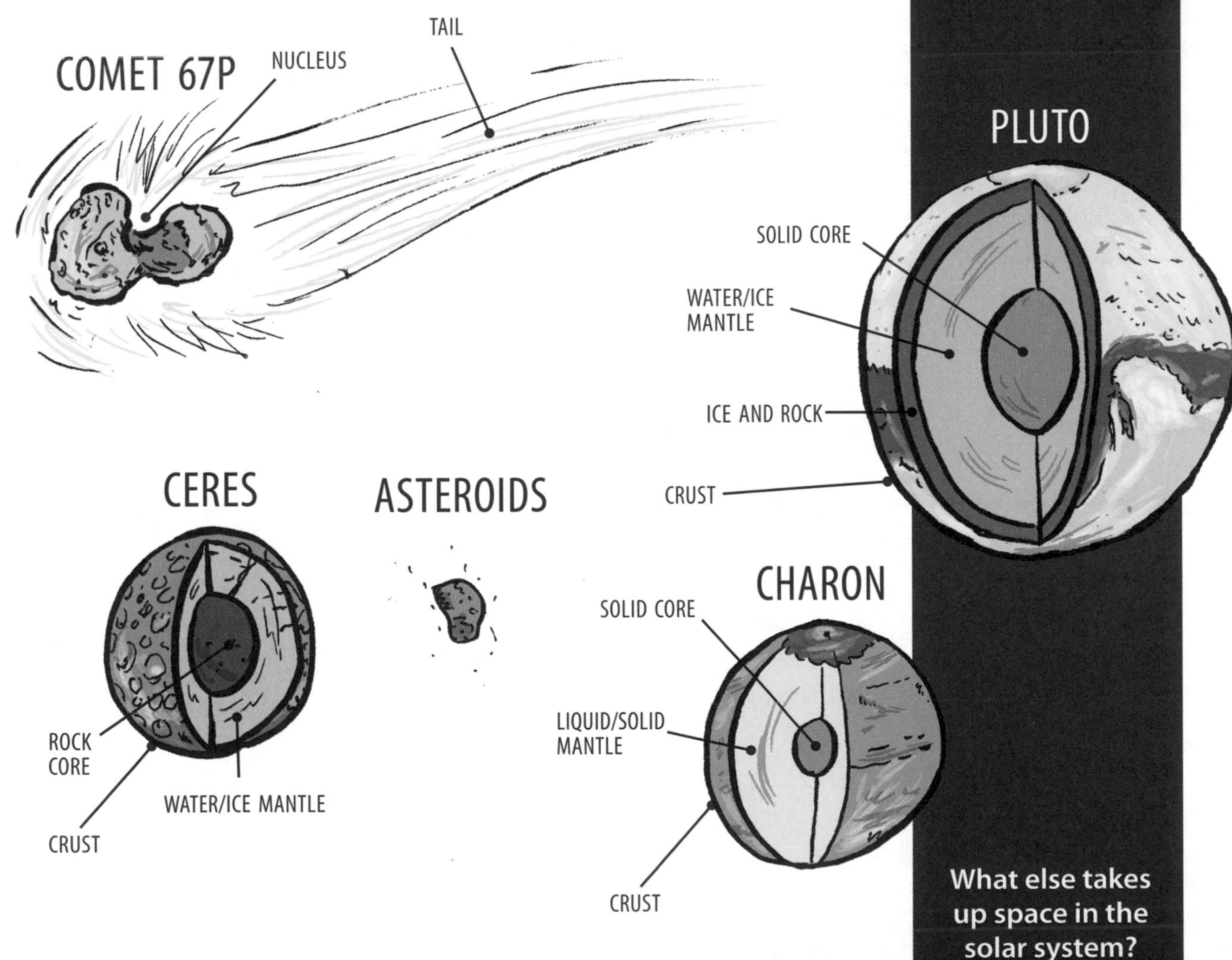

What else takes up space in the solar system?

Besides planets and stars, the solar system contains many other types of celestial objects, including dwarf planets, asteroids, and comets.

Our solar system is home to more than the just the sun and eight planets. Dwarf planets, asteroids, and comets all formed alongside the larger planets, interacting with themselves and other objects for billions of years. Just as with the planets, the objects closer to the sun are rockier and denser, while those in the outer solar system and beyond are made of ice and dust.

Asteroids and comets have left their scars on the terrestrial planets, their impacts obvious on the smaller worlds but not as visible on Earth and Venus. Dwarf planets, a new category of solar system objects, are very much worlds of their own and have only recently been explored. Despite their size, these smaller members of the solar system are fascinating places and can tell us a lot about the larger planets that often overshadow them.

ASTEROID FACTS

Throughout the solar system, as many as 1 million small, dark pieces of debris known as asteroids orbit the sun. Fragments of the early solar system, these ancient pieces of rubble mostly reside between Mars and Jupiter in an area called the asteroid belt. But not all them are in the asteroid belt! There are some that lead and follow Jupiter in its orbit, where the gravitational force of the planet and the sun balance each other. Others occasionally make their way to the inner planets, including Earth.

While they might seem like simple space rocks, how and why asteroids formed is still something of a mystery. They could be the leftovers of a failed planet, broken apart by Jupiter's intense gravity. Or, Jupiter could have simply kept a planet from forming, leaving the planetary building blocks in the asteroid belt to occasionally bump into each other and into other planets.

Several spacecraft have recently visited asteroids, and their observations have begun to unravel the history of many of these mysterious objects.

Mostly small and dark, the asteroids in the asteroid belt are between two and four times more distant from the sun than Earth. Asteroids aren't easy to classify. They can range in size from a few miles across to the width of Texas, and can have almost any shape.

CHANCE OF IMPACT

Although the chance of a large impact today is extremely small, it isn't zero. NASA's Center for Near Earth Object Studies searches for and studies asteroids and other objects that cross Earth's orbit and might someday pose a threat to the planet. More than 10,000 near-Earth objects have been cataloged so far, but none of them pose a serious threat. You can read more about the near-Earth program at this website.

PS

near earth NASA

Hunting for Meteorites

Meteorites can be found all over the earth, if you know how to look for them. Check out this link to see how professional meteorite hunters find their space rocks!

To figure out what asteroids are made of, scientists use a spectrometer to see how light is reflected off their surfaces. Different materials reflect light in different ways, and by studying these patterns, scientists can determine their composition. But spectrometers are only good for analyzing the surface of asteroids. To look inside them, scientists use asteroid fragments found on Earth, called meteorites.

Have you ever seen a shooting star? As objects travel around the solar system, they often leave behind bits and pieces of themselves called meteoroids. When meteoroids enter Earth's atmosphere at tremendous speeds, they usually vaporize in brilliant streaks of light called meteors. Most meteors are so small they never make it to the ground, but when they do, they're called meteorites.

By examining these rocks from space, planetary scientists can classify most of them into three general categories.

- **C-type (carbon-rich) asteroids:** Mostly made of clay, rocks, and carbon compounds. These are the most common type of asteroid and are generally found in the outer region of the asteroid belt.
- **S-type (stony) asteroids:** Mostly made of rock mixed with nickel and iron, these asteroids tend to orbit in the middle of the asteroid belt.
- **M-type (metallic) asteroids:** The rarest asteroids, thought to be made almost entirely of metals, including nickel and iron. They usual orbit on the inner edge of the asteroid belt.

Most meteorites are pieces of stony and metallic asteroids, but some are from the moon—and even Mars!

Most asteroids are well behaved in their orbits, but close encounters with other objects can send them off in unpredictable directions, even toward Earth.

About 50,000 years ago, an asteroid moving 10 times faster than a bullet slammed into the region now known as northern Arizona. It left a crater more than 1 mile across and 560 feet deep, and sent molten rock and debris raining across the desert.

In 2013, a meteor exploded in the sky over the city of Chelyabinsk, Russia, shattering windows for miles around. Geologists and paleontologists are fairly certain that an asteroid is to blame for the extinction of the dinosaurs.

About 65 million years ago, an object approximately 6 miles across hit Earth, casting huge amounts of dust into the sky and causing temperatures to drop around the world. Geologists believe this was the beginning of the end for the dinosaurs.

Meteorite crater, Arizona

photo credit: Ken Thomas

PS

CERES: ASTEROID OR DWARF PLANET?

While most of the objects in the asteroid belt are small, oddly shaped chunks of rock and dust, there's one that stands out from the rest. At different times, it's been labeled a planet, a minor planet, an asteroid, and a dwarf planet. An amazing spacecraft, *Dawn*, has recently arrived to study it.

Even with its new status as a dwarf planet, Ceres still gets to keep its title of largest asteroid.

Ceres was discovered in 1801. At the time, many astronomers felt that the large gap between Mars and Jupiter must be hiding a planet. They devoted many hours to hunting for one. Finally, Italian astronomer Giuseppe Piazzi spied a small, faint object that briefly replaced Jupiter as the fifth planet from the sun. However, the membership of Ceres in the planet club didn't last long.

Image of Ceres from *Dawn*, 2015

photo credit: NASA/JPL-Caltech/UCLA/MPS/DLR/IDA

Shortly after its discovery, other small objects were found in the same area, suddenly making the solar system seem crowded. Astronomers realized that there might be dozens of these small objects, and to separate them from the "true" planets, they became known as asteroids, with Ceres simply being the largest. In 2006, the status of Ceres changed again, thanks to formal definitions of planets and dwarf planets.

As a small and distant dwarf planet, Ceres appears as little more than a small dot even through the best telescopes. Ceres orbits the sun at an average distance of 2.76 AU, which puts it roughly in the middle of the asteroid belt.

> Ceres takes 4.6 Earth years to complete one orbit around the sun. With a tilt of just 3 degrees, it doesn't have seasons, but its orbit is elliptical enough that there are slight changes in temperature depending on its distance from the sun.

Ceres is also a quickly spinning world. A day on Ceres lasts just 9.07 hours. And while the dwarf planet is massive enough to pull itself into a sphere, at just 590 miles across, it's only one-third the size of the moon and much less dense. An astronaut standing on the surface would weigh just 1⁄36 of their Earth weight.

For more than 200 years after its discovery, not much else was known about the largest asteroid, but in 2015, NASA'S *Dawn* spacecraft became the first probe to see the dwarf planet up close. The mission revealed that it's more like the terrestrial planets than neighboring asteroids.

MINING ASTEROIDS

Would you like to be an asteroid miner? Governments and companies are interested in mining asteroids for valuable metals, such as platinum. Check out Deep Space Industries here.

Deep Space Industries

EXPLORING CERES

SPACE ELEMENT

Before reaching Ceres, *Dawn* visited Vesta—the second-largest object in the asteroid belt.

As *Dawn* approached Ceres, scientists weren't sure what they'd find. The first pictures from the probe revealed a surface with thousands of shallow craters, covered in a fine layer of dust. Inside some of these craters, bright spots immediately stood out against the dark surface. These spots puzzled planetary scientists, who first suspected them to be exposed water ice. But with a surface temperature of -36 degrees Fahrenheit (-38 degrees Celsius), water ice in the vacuum of space is warm enough to sublimate, or turn directly from a solid to a gas.

It's suspected that water mixed with magnesium sulfate and other salts makes its way to the surface. As the water disappears, it leaves behind these bright deposits.

> Although Ceres has no atmosphere, *Dawn* detected water vapor near the surface, suggesting that water erupts from deep below the surface.

Ceres's interior is more like that of Jupiter's largest moons than the other asteroids. Measurements of the dwarf planet's weak gravity hint at a solid, rocky core covered by a large mantle of water ice. If that's true, the mantle could hold more water than all of Earth! However, planetary scientists aren't sure how these frozen ices make their way to the surface through cracks and vents. Ceres is so small that scientists predicted it was frozen solid, and there's no large planet nearby to squeeze it, as Jupiter squeezes Io and Europa. It's a mystery that scientists hope *Dawn* will help solve.

WHAT'S NEXT

There's still a lot to learn about asteroids and their place in the solar system. The *Dawn* spacecraft continues to study Ceres in great detail, sending back images of its surface and information about its interior. Planetary scientists want to learn more about its formation and the possibility of an underground ocean, as well as the bright deposits on the surface.

Two new missions have been designed to explore some objects both inside and outside the asteroid belt. *Lucy* is a mission to inspect a group of asteroids that have a unique position outside of the asteroid belt. The Trojan asteroids share Jupiter's orbit in two groups, one ahead and one behind the giant planet.

The *Psyche* mission will meet up with an interesting asteroid named 16 Psyche. About 130 miles wide, Psyche is thought to be made almost entirely of iron and nickel. It might be the remains of a core of a planet that was ripped apart billions of years ago by collisions with other proto-planets. Studying it would give planetary scientists new insights into how planets are formed and what their cores are really like. Both missions are scheduled for the early 2020s.

The Trojans are thought to be remnants left over from the creation of the giant planets, and might hold clues to help understand their formation.

THE KUIPER BELT

Beyond the orbit of Neptune is a collection of small bodies left over from the formation of the solar system. Like asteroids, these objects never formed a planet, but they can show us what the early outer solar system was like. Called the Kuiper belt, this region stretches from Neptune's orbit to more than 50 AU from the sun. About 20 times wider than the asteroid belt, this large area might contain more than 100 times the mass of all the asteroids combined.

The Kuiper belt objects, also called Trans-Neptunian objects, range in size from boulders to small worlds more than 1,200 miles wide. While there could be more than 100,000 Kuiper belt objects larger than 60 miles across, only about 1,000 have been identified.

At such great distances, Kuiper belt objects are very hard to spot and even harder to study. From what scientists can tell, most are made of water ice, ammonia, and other hydrocarbons mixed with dust and rocks. Many follow long, elliptical orbits with periods measured that stretch into centuries. Most of these cold and distant objects are only a few miles across, but there are a few that stand out, including one that used to be a planet.

How Bright is the Sun?

Just how dim is the light of the sun from Pluto? Living at the edge of the solar system means that the dwarf planet receives much less light than we do on Earth—about 1,500 times less than noon on Earth! But surprisingly, it is still much brighter than the light reflected from the full moon. To experience what high noon might look like on Pluto, check out this website to find when the light where you live is the same as Pluto at noon!

NASA Pluto time

PLUTO FACTS

After Neptune was found using the irregularities of Uranus's orbit, astronomers wondered if another planet might be hidden even farther from the sun, tugging at the ice giants with its gravity. In 1930, Clyde Tombaugh found Pluto, which quickly became the newest planet. But Pluto was tiny and distant and had a very eccentric orbit. The existence of Pluto didn't explain what seemed to be happening to Neptune and its orbit.

About 60 years later, better measurements of Neptune's mass showed that there was no larger object affecting its orbit. Pluto remained the ninth planet for a while longer. Although now classified as a dwarf planet and the largest Kuiper belt object, its visit by the *New Horizons* spacecraft in 2015 proved that Pluto isn't just another ball of ice and dust in the shadows of the solar system.

Pluto's diameter of 1,500 miles makes it smaller than the planet Mercury and smaller than many moons, including ours. Its day is long, lasting 6.38 Earth days. With its axis tipped at 120 degrees, the distant sun rises in the west and sets in the east.

Pluto's path through the solar system is unlike those of any of the eight planets. For 20 years, its elliptical orbit brings it closer to the sun than Neptune, but it spends most of its 248-year-long path far beyond the eighth planet. At its most distant, Pluto is 7 billion miles from the sun, almost 50 times the distance between Earth and the sun. This huge elliptical orbit is also inclined at 17 degrees to the plane of the solar system. This carries Pluto slightly above and below the larger bodies of the solar system, depending on where it is in its trip around the sun.

Pluto was named after the Roman god of the underworld. The name was suggested in 1930 by an 11-year-old girl named Venetia Burney.

EXPLORING PLUTO

In 2015, the first spacecraft to visit a Kuiper belt object passed by Pluto on its way out of the solar system. The *New Horizons* probe examined Pluto in great detail as it sped by after nearly a decade of travel, capturing fantastic images of Pluto's surface, moons, and atmosphere.

Pluto has a very thin nitrogen atmosphere that rises an incredible 1,000 miles into space, but produces a surface pressure of only a few millionths of Earth's atmospheric pressure at sea level. This is much less than at the top of even Earth's tallest mountains.

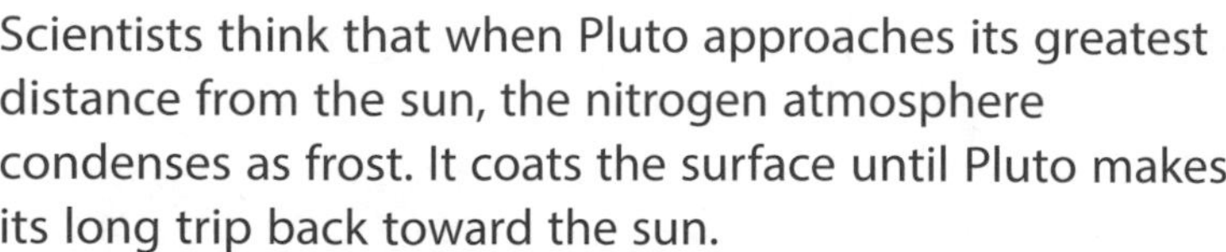

Scientists think that when Pluto approaches its greatest distance from the sun, the nitrogen atmosphere condenses as frost. It coats the surface until Pluto makes its long trip back toward the sun.

New Horizons found Pluto's surface to be covered in an incredible variety of terrain, with soaring mountains made of water ice, large craters, and smooth planes. The dwarf planet's reddish-brown coloring comes from tholins, a kind of tar-like substance created through the interaction of sunlight and chemicals such as methane and nitrogen. A large, heart-shaped area named Tombaugh Regio consists of craterless plains covered in layers of frozen nitrogen, carbon monoxide, and other ices.

What's In A Name?

Although not yet official, the surface features of Pluto have many names associated with the god of the underworld. But there a number of places with names of famous explorers, authors, scientists, and engineers—and even some from science fiction and fantasy! Check out some of the proposed names here.

names for Pluto's features

> With so few craters, Tombaugh Regio might be less than 100,000 million years old and offers evidence of a warm, liquid ocean beneath the frozen surface.

Before *New Horizons*, Pluto was thought to consist of a solid ball of ice around a small core of rock and metal. But with so many areas of young terrain, scientists are confident that the rocky core is surrounded by a planet-wide ocean supporting a crust of water ice.

DOUBLE DWARF PLANETS

The most famous dwarf planet also hosts five moons: Charon, Hydra, Nix, Styx, and Kerberos. Charon's diameter of 800 miles makes it more than half the size of Pluto, and the duo are sometimes called a binary dwarf planet.

New Horizons was able to photograph only one side of Charon during its 31,000-mile-per-hour visit, but even that one view has scientists puzzled. A massive canyon more than 621 miles long and twice as deep as the Grand Canyon stretches across the surface, looking like an ugly scar. A red cap of tholins decorates Charon's north pole, thought to be deposited there by Pluto's loose and tenuous atmosphere.

While Charon is large enough to be a dwarf planet on its own, the other four moons are tiny, oddly shaped clumps of rock and ice. The largest is no bigger than 19 miles across.

The distance between Pluto (on the right) and Charon is not to scale in this picture.

photo credit: NASA/JHUAPL/SwRI

PS

After its encounter with Pluto and Charon, *New Horizons* is off to study a much smaller Kuiper belt object sometime in 2019. But planetary scientists on Earth are still gathering data on the other dwarf planets in the Kuiper belt—Haumea, Makemake, and Eris.

THE OUTER DWARF PLANETS

When it was discovered in 2003, Eris caused a lot of problems. For one, it appeared to be about the same size as Pluto, possibly making it the 10th planet. But its orbit was even less like the other planets than Pluto's, taking it as far as 97 AU on an orbit tilted 44 degrees from the rest of the solar system.

In 2005, the two more large Kuiper belt objects were detected. Scientists wondered how many more bodies like Pluto there might be in huge, tilted orbits, and if they could really be considered planets. In 2006, the IAU finally decided that a formal definition of a planet was needed. Because, like Ceres, Pluto, Haumea, Makemake, and Eris were unable to clear their orbits of other objects, they became the five dwarf planets.

Little is known about these distant members of the solar system. Accompanied by its moon Dysnomia, Eris takes nearly 560 years to orbit the sun. Makemake, estimated to be 870 miles wide, has one tiny, unnamed moon and takes 310 years to complete one trip around the sun. And the egg-shaped Haumea, 1,200 miles across at its widest, is followed by its two moons, Hi'aka and Namaka. Together, they orbit the sun in about 285 years.

Because these objects are so small and distant, it's possible there are other dwarf planets in even stranger orbits waiting to be found. They could even have orbits that take them much further away from the sun, maybe even to the edge of the Oort Cloud.

Comets Can Make an Impact

When a comet strays too close to a planet, the planet's gravity can alter its course. In the case of comet Shoemaker-Levy 9, Jupiter's gravity steered it into a collision course with the planet itself in 1994! What do you think would happen if Shoemaker-Levy had hit the earth instead? Check out this clip.

History Channel Shoemaker-Levy

COMETS AND THE OORT CLOUD

Far beyond the orbits of Pluto and the other Kuiper belt objects lies the realm of comets. Named after Danish astronomer Jan Oort (1900–1992), the Oort Cloud surrounds the entire solar system like a bubble, stretching from 5,000 to more than 100,000 AU. It's so incredibly far from Earth that *Voyager 2*, traveling more than 1 million miles a day, won't reach even the inner edge for another 300 years. It's a vast area, thought to hold trillions of icy objects left over from the early solar nebula.

Occasionally, something nudges one of these small and distant objects, sending it on a long trip to the inner solar system. We call these visitors comets.

For thousands of years, ancient people feared and worshipped the unpredictable appearance of comets. Comets are small bodies made mostly of ice and dust left over from the formation of the solar system. Coated in dark grey organic material, they look like asteroids, but their compositions and origins are very different. Like asteroids, comets are time capsules from the early solar nebula, but having formed so far from the center of the solar system, they've recorded a colder and more distant history.

In the past, most comets were named after their discoverers, such as Halley's Comet and comet Shoemaker-Levy 9. Now that many spacecraft and telescopes are finding lots of comets, they're given the names of the instruments used to spot them.

Although about 4,000 comets are known, some estimates predict more than 100 billion comets might be scattered in the Oort Cloud.

COMETS

Many early astronomers kept meticulous records of comets, recording their movements and illustrating their appearances in different forms of art. Today, comets are known as the most distant remnants from the early solar system, having changed little in 4.6 billion years. Made of ice and dust, these dirty snowballs might have helped bring water and the building blocks of life to the planets and moons of the solar system.

Comets often have extremely elliptical and often tilted orbits that can take them out to more than 50,000 AU from the sun with periods that can last hundreds, thousands, and even hundreds of thousands of years. Occasionally, a comet's orbit is changed by chance encounters with other objects, sending them toward the sun. As they make their way into the inner solar system, these sleepy snowballs spring to life, growing tails of dust and plasma that can light up the night sky.

EXPLORING COMETS

While most comets never make it into the inner solar system, those that do often put on a spectacular show. All comets have a nucleus, or center. Usually only a few miles across, the nucleus is made of water ice mixed with gas and dust. As it approaches the sun, the ice and gas begin to heat up, giving the comet a kind of atmosphere, called a coma. Depending on the comet and its distance from the sun, the coma can grow to be hundreds of miles long, sometimes splitting into separate tails of gas and dust. The slight pressure of sunlight steers the tails so that they always point away from the sun. Although unpredictable, comets with enough ice and gas can easily be seen from Earth.

Most comets that enter the inner solar system make their way out, but some have a different fate. Called sun-grazing comets, these unlucky representatives from the outer solar system either crash directly into the sun or are torn apart by the intense heat and radiation.

Many space probes have visited comets while on their journeys through the solar system. The most recent was the ESA's *Rosetta* and *Philae* mission to Comet 67P/Churyumov–Gerasimenko. Shaped like a peanut, Comet 67P is a comet with an orbit of only 20 years, making it an excellent object to study.

The first probe to orbit and land on a comet, *Rosetta/Philae* returned spectacular images and science data for two years, leading scientists to discover that comets are much less dense than they'd originally thought. The spacecraft also detected elements essential to life, suggesting that comets might have brought these necessary chemicals to Earth early on in the planet's formation.

The *Rosetta* and *Philae* mission ended in 2016, with *Rosetta* taking a sharp dive into the comet. The plume of debris from its impact was visible to telescopes from Earth, giving scientists another look at the innerworkings of Comet 67P.

While there are no new missions planned for comets, plenty of scientists have made interesting proposals. One mission calls for a "hopper" to travel across a comet by making small jumps in the meager gravity, collecting and analyzing samples from different environments on the comet's surface.

Still others are calling for a spacecraft to take a sample directly from the comet's nucleus and return it to Earth to be examined in detail. And with *New Horizons* on its way to meet up with another Kuiper belt object in 2019, we'll soon have a chance to learn even more about these icy worlds at the edge of the solar system.

VOCAB LAB 

Write down what you think each word means. What root words can you find that will help?

asteroid belt, **meteor**, **meteorite**, **meteoroid**, **Kuiper belt**, **vaporize**, **demote**, **tholin**, **sublimate**, **coma**, and **sun-grazing comets**.

Compare your definitions with those of your friends or classmates. Did you all come up with the same meanings? Turn to the text and glossary if you need help.

KEY QUESTIONS

- **Have you ever seen a meteorite or a comet? What do you think people in ancient times felt when they saw these bright things in the sky?**
- **Why is it important to have clear definitions of planets, dwarf planets, and asteroids?**

SCALE MODELS OF THE DWARF PLANETS

While they're not full-fledged planets, dwarf planets are still members of the solar system! Just as with other far-away celestial objects, building a scale model can help us better understand their motions and places in the solar system.

- **Choose at least two different dwarf planets to model.** Consider what materials you might use to get started.
- **Only Ceres and Pluto have been studied up close.** How can you use your knowledge of these worlds to help understand the ones we've yet to visit?
- **Using your scale size, how large would the orbits be for your dwarf planet models?** Bigger than your house, your neighborhood, or your city?

To investigate more, compare your dwarf planets to your other solar system objects. Are they similar in size? How does your choice of scale size affect each set of models? Can you build a model solar system that includes all the planets and dwarf planets?

SPACE ELEMENT

The largest model of the solar system is in Stockholm, Sweden. The sun is modeled by the dome of the Globe Arena, the largest spherical structure in the world, and is more than 44 feet wide. At this scale, Pluto is a small sphere about 5 inches wide, and is in the town of Delsbo—more than 186 miles away!

ASTEROIDS MAKE IMPACT

Lots of planets and moons in the solar system show battle scars from ancient asteroid impacts. But on Earth, they're hard to find. Millions of years of rain and wind have erased much of the evidence, but there are still plenty of craters left, if you know where to look.

The Earth Impact Database has an interactive map of crater sites all over the world. Check out this website and explore.

Earth Impact Database

- **Do some research and compare and contrast two or more craters on Earth.** You could use a Venn diagram, a table, or other method to express the information you gather.
- **What kinds of things affect the size and shape of craters.** What affects their impact sites?
- **How different are craters on the moon, Earth, and Mars?** What do you think causes these differences?
- **Are there are any craters near you?** Go visit one!

To investigate more, consider what would happen if an asteroid struck the ocean, your country, or even your hometown. This simulator lets you adjust the size, composition, and speed of an object, and send it on a collision course with Earth.

asteroid simulator

Inquire & Investigate

CREATE YOUR OWN COMET

In the outer solar system, ice becomes the building blocks of comets, which are called "dirty iceballs" for a good reason. Comets are mostly water ice mixed with dust and dirt. These are materials we have plenty of right here on Earth!

- **Create your own comet.** What materials do you think you could use? How do your materials represent the real structure of comets?
- **Model your comet.** What shape will your comet take? Will it have coma, or tails?
- **Don't forget to name your comet!** What have been some sources of names for objects in our solar system?

To investigate more, check out this video from the NASA Jet Propulsion Laboratory on how to make your own comet using dry ice! Always have an adult help with handling dangerous substances.

dry ice comet YouTube

Chapter 6

Exoplanets and Planet 9

What lies at the edge of the solar system and beyond?

It's very difficult to study the regions beyond the ice giants, but we have found evidence of exoplanets out there, perhaps even ones that orbit a star.

Are there other planets out there? With billions of stars in our galaxy, it seems impossible that our solar system could be the only one. Until relatively recently, astronomers couldn't say for sure if there were other worlds beyond our own. But in the last 25 years, the tools needed to detect and study these worlds have become more powerful, leading to some amazing results.

There are now more than 3,500 confirmed exoplanets orbiting distant stars and more are being discovered all the time. While there are some planets that can be considered Earth-like, many of them are large, hot worlds in orbits very different from the paths our familiar planets take. But we might not need to look too far for other planets. There's strong evidence for an exoplanet around the nearest star to our own and there might even be another planet hiding within our solar system.

THE HUNT FOR PLANET 9

The hunt for hidden planets in the solar system has had some hits and misses. The search for a planet between Mars and Jupiter led to the discovery of Ceres and the asteroid belt, while the movements of Uranus led to the prediction and discovery of Neptune. But the hunt for a world beyond Neptune has had mixed results. While the discovery of Pluto temporarily gave astronomers their ninth planet, it wasn't the large object they thought they'd find. The discovery of more Kuiper belt objects beyond Pluto helped revive a search that many thought was over.

While studying the orbits of Kuiper belt objects, astronomers noticed that their orbits tend to line up in ways that seem unlikely to happen by chance. By using computer simulations to model different possibilities, the astronomers determined that a large planet on a very long and elliptical orbit might be having an effect on these smaller worlds.

Being scientists, they were skeptical. Could there really be a large, undiscovered planet? Still not convinced, they used their results to predict the presence of another group of objects affected by this mysterious world—and found them. In 2015, astronomers Konstantin Batygin and Mike Brown announced they'd found strong evidence for a ninth planet, hidden near the edge of the solar system.

Join the Hunt

Do you want to help look for Planet 9? Science needs your help! Looking for very dim objects deep in the solar system is a difficult job. Lots of pictures need to be looked at, more than astronomers can handle themselves! Follow the link to help in the search for a possible new planet in our solar system!

Planet 9 might even be a rogue planet, a world without a sun drifting through the cosmos and captured as it passed our solar system.

Because Planet 9 is only a possibility, it's hard to know what it might be like. But astronomers have a few good guesses. Based on its effect on other objects, Planet 9 is probably a large world, between 10 and 20 times Earth's mass. Such a large world is likely to be an ice giant like Uranus or Neptune instead of a rocky world like Earth. At its closest, this far-away world would still be seven times farther from the sun than Neptune, and at its most distant it could be more than 1,000 AU from the sun.

But where could it have come from? Planetary scientists believe that so far out in the solar nebula, it's very difficult for large worlds to grow. Instead, Planet 9 might have formed much closer to the sun, only to be cast out when it came too close to another planet's gravitational influence. Another theory is that while all the planets in our solar system formed together more than 4.6 billion years ago, Planet 9 might have a very different origin. The potential world could have been captured from a passing solar system that crossed paths with ours millions or even billions of years ago.

Rogue Planets

Astronomers think that most rogue planets began life in a solar system, only to be ejected by the gravity of another world. It's also possible that they simply formed from a much smaller cloud of dust and debris that just wasn't large enough to create a star in the first place. These homeless worlds might wander the galaxy, unless they're captured by the gravity of a passing star.

If Planet 9 exists, and if it's not an original member of the solar system, then it just might be the nearest exoplanet to Earth.

If there's a world at the edge of our solar system, why haven't we seen it yet? The simplest answer is that anything so cold and distant would be extremely difficult to detect, even with the best equipment. And if Planet 9 is at or near its farthest distance from the sun, it could be moving so slowly that finding it in the darkness of the outer solar system would be almost impossible—unless you knew where to look.

By knowing its likely path, astronomers have narrowed down Planet 9's possible locations in the sky. They are using some of the largest, most sensitive telescopes in the world to search for it. Because all the data seems to be pointing toward this hidden world being real, scientists hope that they'll have the first direct proof of its existence very soon!

EXOPLANETS

Until recently, planetary scientists weren't sure if there were planets orbiting other suns. It seemed reasonable to think there would be—with at least 100 billion stars in the Milky Way galaxy, surely some of them must have a planet or two. But as with Planet 9 and other distant objects, finding them isn't easy.

Astronomers estimate there could be as many as 100 billion planets in the Milky Way.

An artist's concept of Kepler-47

photo credit: NASA Ames/JPL-Caltech/T. Pyle

SPACE ELEMENT

In 1995, the first exoplanet around a sun-like star was found using Doppler spectroscopy. This planet, named 51 Pegasi b, is considered a hot Jupiter, a gas giant that closely orbits its star. It's so close that its orbit takes only four days, and the temperature at its cloud tops is around 1,832 degrees Fahrenheit (1,000 degrees Celsius)!

WOBBLE

For an illustration of how the wobble of a star affects its light, check out this video.

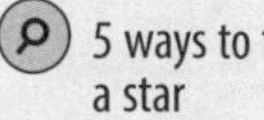

5 ways to find a star

Even the nearest star, Proxima Centauri, is so far away that any planet circling it would be lost in its intense glare. But in 1995, the first planet orbiting a sun-like star was found, not by looking directly for a planet, but by studying its star.

Although we talk about planets orbiting stars, this isn't exactly right. Stars and planets actually orbit a point in space where the gravitational force of both is balanced. This is called the barycenter. Because a star is more massive than a planet, the barycenter is usually much closer to the star, and sometimes even inside of it. As both objects swing around this common center, the planet moves in its larger orbit while the star appears to wobble slightly.

> The wobble produces a change in the star's light, called a Doppler shift.

The light from a star appears more blue as it's moving toward us, and more red as it moves away. By measuring how much the light shifts, astronomers can determine a potential exoplanet's mass, orbital period, and distance from its star.

The first planet discovered orbiting a sun-like star was found using this method, and it's been used to detect many others. But it does have some limitations. Doppler spectroscopy is a great way to find giant planets that closely orbit their stars because their gravitational forces create a bigger wobble. But planets such as Earth pull much more gently on their stars and are much harder to detect. And if the orbit of the planet isn't lined up just right, we might not see the wobble at all. Fortunately, there are a few other ways to hunt down these alien worlds.

Another way to look for exoplanets is to look for their shadows. As the moon passes between the sun and Earth during a solar eclipse, it can block some or all of the sun's light, casting a shadow. Venus and Mercury can also pass between the sun and Earth, but because they're much farther away, the effect is less dramatic. This is called a transit.

When an exoplanet passes between us and its star, it causes a very small but measurable "dip" in the star's brightness. Because there are other things that can cause a star to dim, astronomers have to see if the change in the star's light repeats itself.

Sunspots, as well as clouds of interstellar dust and gas, can all cause the amount of light from a star to change, but if a pattern of dimming occurs, it could signal the presence of a planet. Observing these tiny changes in a star's brightness requires very sensitive telescopes with excellent seeing conditions, preferably one that can watch stars for years at a time.

Fortunately, astronomers have the Kepler Space Telescope. In 2009, the Kepler Space Telescope left Earth to look for transiting exoplanets, free from the blurring effects of Earth's atmosphere. Kepler stares continuously at one patch of sky, observing more than 100,000 stars at once in hopes of seeing the tell-tale sign of a transit. So far, Kepler has detected more than 2,300 confirmed exoplanets, with thousands more waiting for confirmation. Thanks to the Kepler Space Telescope, astronomers believe that planets are common in the universe, and that all stars probably have at least one planet.

While Doppler spectroscopy and detecting transits help find planets, they can't tell us much about the planets' atmospheres, their surfaces, or if they have life. To do so, astronomers will need to see the planets directly.

Although our eyes can't detect small changes in the amount of light from a star, very sensitive instruments can, even if the star and planet are very far away!

A Planet with Two Suns

The discovery of Kepler 16b in 2011 was exciting for scientists and sci-fi fans. Nicknamed Tatooine, Kepler 16b orbits two suns, just like the planet in the *Star Wars* universe. Kepler 16b seems to be about the size of Saturn and makes one orbit every 229 days. Because both of its stars are much dimmer than ours, Kepler 16b is probably a cold and frozen world, but the sunsets would still be spectacular!

Sacred Ground

To reduce the blurring effects of Earth's atmosphere, the largest telescopes are often built in the thin air of mountaintops. Many of these mountains are sacred to indigenous peoples, and there are sometimes disputes over the use of these sites. The construction of the giant Thirty Meter Telescope, originally planned to be built on the ancient volcano Mauna Kea in Hawaii, has angered many Hawaiians. How would you balance science with these sacred locations? You can read more about it here.

PS

NY Times Hawaii telescope

DIRECT IMAGING

Can we see planets around other stars? So far, most exoplanets have been discovered indirectly. Because planets are so much dimmer than the stars they orbit, detecting even the faintest amount of light from an exoplanet is extremely hard. But recent advances in technology are starting to bring some of these planets into focus.

If you've ever noticed the twinkling of stars on a dark night, you've seen one of the biggest problems with telescopes on Earth. As light from a star passes through the atmosphere, turbulent air causes the stars to twinkle. It blurs their images, even in the largest telescopes.

To fight this twinkling, astronomers are using adaptive optics to counteract the blurring and create amazingly clear images. Using a laser, computer software monitors how the light changes as it passes through the atmosphere and makes tiny adjustments to the telescope's mirrors. These flexible mirrors help sharpen the image and bring out faint details.

To really see the faint light from planets, astronomers need to block as much glare from the star as possible. If you've ever used your hand to block the light of a really bright light, you've used a kind of coronagraph. A coronagraph is an extremely small disk that fits inside a telescope to block the light from a star. Combined with adaptive optics and computer software, a coronagraph makes it possible to see the light reflected from distant planets.

Although seeing these planets directly is still very difficult, astronomers are confident that with the next generations of telescopes on Earth and in space, we'll be able to see more exoplanets in orbit around their stars.

Planets in Motion Around

During the course of six years, astronomers from the Keck observatory in Hawaii observed the star HR 8799 and managed to capture four planets in orbit around it. Astronomers hope to study the system in the future to determine if any of the planets could support life. You can watch the video of the planets at this website.

NASA four planets orbit

A PLANET AROUND THE NEAREST STAR

In 2016, astronomers using the 3.6-meter telescope at La Silla in Chile made an incredible announcement. They'd found a planet circling the star nearest our solar system. Proxima Centauri is a red dwarf, a far smaller and cooler star than our sun. It orbits two larger and brighter stars in a triple star system called Alpha Centauri, the brightest of which is easily visible from the Southern Hemisphere on Earth.

The planet, called Proxima b, is slightly more massive than Earth and orbits Proxima Centauri within the star's habitable zone. Because Proxima Centauri is a red dwarf, it puts out nearly 1,000 times less energy than our sun. As a result, its habitable zone is much smaller and closer to the star than in our solar system. In fact, Proxima b orbits its star 10 times closer than Mercury orbits the sun, and its year is just 11 Earth days long.

To truly understand if Proxima b is habitable, astronomers are looking toward the next generation of planet-hunting telescopes to help analyze its atmosphere and composition.

Being so close to a star has some major disadvantages. Red dwarfs such as Proxima Centauri are thought to have huge solar flares that throw particles and radiation off their surfaces and out into space. A planet that orbits close to a red dwarf could be smothered in dangerous flares, which would boil away water and rip apart the atmosphere. Proxima b would need a strong magnetic field to protect its surface from its parent.

Exploring Proxima b

At 4.2 light-years away, it would take several lifetimes to visit Proxima b in person. But a proposal to send a tiny spacecraft to the Alpha Centauri system might actually work. Using a massive sail and a powerful laser, physicists think they can accelerate an extremely lightweight probe to about one-fifth lightspeed, crossing the distance in just 20 years instead of centuries. Check out this news article to learn more about the *Starshot*.

Wired nano starship

> Could Proxima b be like Earth? That's a difficult question to answer.

We really know only its orbit and mass. Based on what we know about our solar system, it could be either a terrestrial planet or something more like hot Neptune. Orbiting its star so closely, the world probably keeps the same side facing inward, always baking in the solar radiation. How would that affect the planet and any atmosphere or surface it might have?

WHAT'S NEXT FOR EXOPLANETS?

During the next decade, scientists are constructing a number of telescopes with the ability to look for and study exoplanets. The James Webb Space Telescope (JWST) is really, really big. While the Hubble telescope has a 7.9-foot mirror, the JWST's mirror will be more than 21 feet wide, collecting seven times more light than Hubble. In its own orbit around the sun, JWST will analyze the light from exoplanets and determine the compositions of their atmospheres. It could even detect the presence of water and signs of vegetation.

While the Kepler Space Telescope has watched a single patch of stars, a new satellite called the Transiting Exoplanet Survey Satellite (TESS) will survey the entire sky, focusing on stars within 100 light years of Earth. Scientists hope that TESS will observe more than 200,000 stars, watching for signs of a transit. Its measurements will allow astronomers to determine the mass, diameter, and length of year for exoplanets. TESS will provide nearby targets for Earth and space-based telescopes, including JWST, to examine in detail.

One tool might help astronomers see exoplanets directly. Similar to a coronagraph, a starshade blocks the overwhelming light from a star, letting reflected light from any planets to shine through. But instead of being placed inside the telescope, the starshade would sit at a great distance from its space-based telescope in order to change its size and shape for a particular star. The starshade could revolutionize how we study exoplanets. Imagine the worlds that might be discovered!

People have learned a lot about planets in the short time we've been able to study them. There are always new discoveries being made—a new exoplanet, evidence for ancient seas on Mars, or close-up images of Saturn's majestic rings. But there's still so much to learn! Maybe you'll be the one to discover Planet 9, explore the oceans of Europa and Enceladus, or even find life beyond Earth!

KEY QUESTIONS

- What do you think we'll find beyond the boundaries of our solar system?
- Why does the search for Earth-like planets drive much of our space exploration?
- Do you think we'll ever find life on other planets?

VOCAB LAB 

Write down what you think each word means. What root words can you find that will help?

rogue planet, **exoplanet**, **barycenter**, **Doppler shift**, **transit**, **sunspot**, **adaptive optics**, **laser**, **coronagraph**, **red dwarf**, **solar flare**, and **starshade**.

Compare your definitions with those of your friends or classmates. Did you all come up with the same meanings? Turn to the text and glossary if you need help.

Inquire & Investigate

MODEL AN ALIEN PLANET

There are thousands of known exoplanets out there, but what are they like? Some we know little about, while others we understand more.

- **Research an interesting exoplanet.** Does it orbit one star or two? Or three?
- **What kind of world is the exoplanet likely to be?** A rocky world like Earth or a giant ball of gas like Jupiter?
- **Construct your model however you want using any medium you like.** You can make a 3-D model or a drawing.
- **Give your exoplanet surface features.** Be creative—would it be a desert world or an ocean paradise? A small world with a huge ring system or an icy distant world at the edge of its solar system?
- **Explain why you chose your planet.** How did you decide on its features?

To investigate more, consider that many exoplanets are part of a solar system with other planets. Can you build a scale model of an alien solar system? How would it be different from your own solar system? How would it be similar?

CITIZEN SCIENCE

While thousands of exoplanets have been found, many more are waiting to be discovered—and you can help. Scientists often gather more information than they can analyze, but as a citizen scientist, you can help pick up the slack. At this website, you can help look for exoplanets by analyzing the patterns of light recorded by the Kepler Space Telescope.

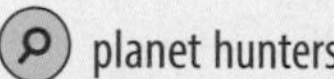

absorb: to soak up a liquid or take in energy, heat, light, or sound.

accretion: the process of particles sticking together to form larger objects, such as planets.

adaptive optics: a system that adjusts a telescope to cancel out the blurring effects of the Earth's atmosphere.

adaptive: the ability to change.

algae: organisms that live in water and can make oxygen through photosynthesis.

ammonia: a colorless, gaseous compound of nitrogen and hydrogen that can easily be condensed by cold and pressure to form a liquid.

asteroid belt: a collection of small, rocky objects that orbit the sun between Mars and Jupiter.

asteroid: small, rocky objects that orbit the sun. Most, but not all, asteroids orbit the sun in the asteroid belt.

astrobiologist: a scientist who studies the origin and evolution of life in the universe.

astronomer: a person who studies the stars, planets, and other bodies in space.

astronomical unit (AU): the average distance between the sun and the Earth, about 93 million miles (150 million kilometers).

astronomy: the study of the stars, planets, and space.

atmosphere: the mixture of gases surrounding a planet.

attribute: a unique feature or characteristic.

axis of rotation: an imaginary line that connects the north and south poles of an object.

axis: an imaginary line down the middle of a sphere, around which it rotates.

bacteria: microscopic, single-celled organisms that can live in many different environments.

barycenter: a location around which two objects orbit each other.

bio-markers: chemical evidence of living organisms.

biology: the study of living things.

canyon: a deep, narrow valley with steep sides.

captured world: an object orbiting a planet that did not originally form with that planet.

carbon dioxide: a gas in the air made of carbon and oxygen atoms.

celestial body: a star, planet, moon, or other object in space.

chaos terrain: area on the surface of an object made of different types of terrain, such as ridges, cracks, and plains jumbled together.

chemistry: the science of how substances interact, combine, and change.

classify: to put things in groups based on what they have in common.

climate change: a change in long-term weather patterns, which can happen through natural or man-made processes.

climate: weather patterns in an area over a long period of time.

coalesce: to come together and make one object out of many.

collision: when one object strikes another.

colonize: to move in and settle an area.

coma: a fuzzy envelope of gas surrounding the nucleus of a comet.

comet: a small, icy object formed in the outer solar system that can emit tails of gas and dust if it approaches the sun.

compound: something made of two or more separate elements.

condense: to change from a gas to a liquid.

convection: in an atmosphere, the act of warmer gases rising while cooler gasses sink.

core: the center of an object.

coronagraph: a part of a telescope that blocks direct light from a star, making it easier to see dimmer objects nearby.

cosmic radiation: radiation that comes from sources other than the sun, such as black holes or supernova.

crater: a round pit in the moon or other celestial body caused by the impact of a meteorite.

cryovolcano: similar to a volcano, but instead of erupting molten rock, cryovolcanoes erupt water, ammonia, methane, or other liquids and ices.

GLOSSARY

debris: scattered pieces of something wrecked or destroyed.

decay: the process of rotting or deteriorating.

deity: a god or goddess.

demote: to lower the standing or status of a person or object.

density: the amount of matter in a given space, or mass divided by volume.

diameter: the distance from one side of a spherical object to the other through its center.

disperse: to spread out or give off.

dominate: having the most influence or power.

Doppler shift: the apparent change in the wavelength, or color, of light depending on an object's motion toward or away from an observer.

Doppler spectroscopy: a method of looking for exoplanets that watches for small wobbles or changes in a star's light produced by an orbiting planet.

dwarf planet: similar to a planet but not massive enough to clear its orbit of other, similar objects.

dynamic: when something is constantly changing.

eclipse: when an object moves through the shadow of a celestial body.

eddy: a circular movement of a liquid or a gas, like a swirl.

ejecta: material thrown out as a result of a meteor impact, often surrounding craters.

element: a substance that is made of one type of atom, such as iron, carbon, or oxygen.

elliptical: shaped like an ellipse, or an oval.

elusive: difficult to find.

emit: to produce or discharge.

erosion: the wearing away of a surface by wind, water, or other processes.

evaporate: the process of a liquid becoming a gas.

evolution: changing gradually through time.

exoplanet: a planet that orbits stars other than our sun.

exosphere: a very thin layer of gas surrounding a planet.

extinct: when all members of a species have died, something that can be caused by natural or man-made processes.

extremophile: an organism that thrives in environments that most other life forms cannot live in.

fissures: a crack or fracture on the surface of an object that can sometimes erupt.

fracture: a broken spot.

geochemistry: a science that deals with the chemical composition of and chemical changes in the solid matter of the earth or a celestial body.

geologist: a scientist who studies the history, structure, and origin of the earth.

geology: the study of the materials and processes that formed the earth, which can be used to study the same processes on other worlds (sometimes called astrogeology).

geyser: a vent or opening in the surface of object that emits water or other hot liquid under pressure.

glacier: a body of ice that slowly moves downhill due to gravity.

gossamer: something that is thin, light, or transparent.

gravitational pull: the force of gravity acting on an object.

gravity: a force that pulls two objects toward each other.

greenhouse effect: a process through which energy from the sun is trapped by a planet's atmosphere, warming the planet.

greenhouse gas: a gas, such as carbon dioxide or methane, that helps an atmosphere trap and retain heat. Greenhouse gases can be natural or man-made.

habitable zone: the distance from a star at which liquid water could exist on a planet's surface. Also called the Goldilocks Zone.

habitat: a plant or animal's home.

heliocentric: a sun-centered model of the solar system.

helium: a colorless gas created in a nuclear reaction in the sun. It is the most common element in the universe after hydrogen.

hemisphere: half a sphere, like half a ball.

hexagon: a six-sided shape.

highlands: mountainous, rocky, and cratered terrain on the moon.

hydrogen: the simplest and most abundant element in the universe. Hydrogen and oxygen are the two elements in water.

hydrologic cycle: a continuous process of circulating water between Earth and its atmosphere through evaporation, condensation, and precipitation.

ice age: a time in history when much of Earth was covered in ice.

inclined: when an object's orbit is tipped or tilted compared to the orbits of other objects.

indigenous people: a group of people with cultural and historical ties to a certain location or area.

infrared: a type of electromagnetic radiation (light) that humans can't see but we feel as heat.

inhospitable: difficult or impossible to support life.

interplanetary: between planets.

Jovian planets: a term for Jupiter, Saturn, Uranus, and Neptune.

landform: a physical feature of a planet's surface, such as a mountain or a valley.

landscape: a large area of land with specific features.

laser: a concentrated source of light made of one wavelength, or color.

lava plain: an area on the surface of an object where lava has cooled and solidified after spreading over the surface.

lava: hot, melted rock that has risen to the surface.

light-year: the distance light travels in one year, about 5.9 trillion miles (9.5 trillion kilometers).

lunar: having to do with the moon.

magma: a mixture of molten, semi-molten, and solid rock beneath Earth's surface.

magnetic field: a force that, on Earth, protects the surface by deflecting solar and cosmic radiation.

magnetometer: an instrument to detect, measure, and record properties of magnetic fields.

mammal: a type of animal, such as a human, dog, or cat. Mammals are usually born live, feed milk to their young, and usually have hair or fur covering most of their skin.

mantle: a layer between the crust of an object and its core that is made of a mixture of solid and liquid materials.

mare: (MAR-eh) large, flat plains on the surface of the moon made from ancient volcanic eruptions.

mass: the amount of matter in an object.

matter: anything that has mass and takes up space.

meager: weak, or a small amount.

meteor: a meteoroid that enters Earth's atmosphere, often causing a bright streak of light as it is vaporized by the heat from friction with the atmosphere. A meteor doesn't reach the surface of Earth.

meteorite: a meteor that makes it all the way to the ground.

meteoroid: a small particle traveling in space, usually made of stone or metal.

meteorology: the scientific study of atmospheres, including weather and climate.

methane: a colorless, odorless greenhouse gas.

meticulous: having great attention to detail.

microscopic: something so small it can be seen only with a microscope.

migration: the movement of a large group of organisms, such as birds, due to changes in the environment.

molecular cloud: an interstellar cloud of gas and dust that becomes dense enough to form molecules within it. Molecular clouds are often the beginnings of stars and solar systems.

molten: when an object such as rock or metal is heated and behaves like a liquid.

moon: a body that orbits an object that is not the sun. A moon is also called a natural satellite.

nitrogen: an element that is a gas in the air on Earth.

GLOSSARY

nuclear fusion: the process of hydrogen converting to helium and releasing energy and light.

nucleus: the solid part of a comet, made of rocks, ice, and dust.

oblate spheroid: the sphere-like shape of a planet that is wider at the equator than at the poles due to rotation.

occultation: when a nearby object (such as a moon or planet) passes between a distant object and an observer, blocking it from view.

opaque: not clear.

orbit: the elliptical or curved path a body takes around an object.

organic compound: a chemical compound that contains the element carbon, which is essential for life as we know it.

organism: any living thing, such as a plant or animal.

paleontologist: a scientist who studies plant and animal fossils.

particle: a tiny piece of matter.

period: the time it takes an object to complete one orbit. If the object orbits the sun it is also called a year.

phases: the change in shape of the illumination of an object.

physics: the science of how matter and energy work together.

planet: an object that orbits a star, has pulled itself into a spherical shape, and has cleared the area around itself of similar objects.

planetary science: the science that deals with the condensed matter (the planets and natural satellites) of the solar system.

planetesimals: small objects formed early in the solar system that are thought to have been the beginning of planets.

plasma: an ionized gas considered the fourth state of matter (solid, liquid, gas, plasma).

plate tectonics: the theory that Earth's crust is made of many pieces, or plates, that slowly move over the mantle.

plates: large pieces of Earth's crust.

predict: to estimate what might happen in the future.

pressure: a continuous force that pushes on an object.

probe: a spaceship or satellite used to explore outer space.

proto-sun: the cloud of dust and gas that became the sun.

radar: a device that detects objects by bouncing microwaves or radio waves off them and measuring how long it takes for the waves to return.

radiation: a form of electromagnetic energy, some forms of which can cause harm to living organisms.

radioactive: to emit energy in the form of particles or radiation.

radiometric dating: a method used to determine the age of Earth by measuring the rate of disintegration of radioactive elements.

red dwarf: a small and relatively cool star.

reflect: to redirect something that hits a surface, such as heat, light, or sound.

regolith: broken rock, dust, or soil that covers solid rock.

remote: distant or hard to reach.

resource: things found in nature, such as wood or gold, that people can use.

resurfacing: providing a new or fresh surface through geological activity.

retrograde rotation: rotating in the opposite direction than normal.

rogue planet: a planet that drifts freely through space instead of orbiting a star.

rotate: to turn on an axis.

rover: a slow-moving vehicle used to explore planets.

satellite: natural satellites are also called moons. Artificial satellites are space telescopes, communication satellites, and spaceships.

scarp: a geologic feature with a steep slope that resembles a step.

science fiction: stories that deal with the influence of real or imagined science.

searing: extremely hot.

sedimentary rock: rock that has been formed in layers through flowing water or wind.

seismometer: an instrument used to detect and record movement and vibration in the earth or other objects. Also called a seismograph.

shepherd moon: a small natural satellite that clears a gap in planetary ring material or keeps particles within a ring contained.

silicate: minerals that contain mostly silicon and oxygen.

skeptical: a questioning attitude.

solar flare: electromagnetic energy suddenly released by a star.

solar nebula: a collection of dust and gas that eventually forms a solar system.

solar system: consists of at least one star and all the things that orbit it, such as planets, asteroids, moons, and comets.

space race: the competition between the United States and Soviet Union to have the strongest space program.

species: a group of plants or animals that are similar and can reproduce.

spectrometer: an instrument used to study the properties of light.

sphere: a round object, such as a ball.

starshade: a proposed instrument to block the light from a star so that a space-based telescope can see potential exoplanets.

sublimate: the transition of a substance from a solid to a gas without becoming a liquid.

sulfur dioxide: a toxic gas that can occur in volcanic eruptions.

sun-grazing comets: comets that pass within 850,000 miles (1.38 million kilometers) of the sun.

sunspot: a relatively cool area on the surface of a star that appears dark against the brighter, hotter areas.

supernova: the explosion of a star at the end of its life.

tectonics: the geologic process of changing large areas, or plates, of a planet's surface.

tenuous: thin, weak, or slight.

terrestrial planets: meaning "Earth-like," they are the four planets closest to the sun: Mercury, Venus, Earth and Mars.

theory: an unproven idea used to explain something.

thermal: energy in the form of heat.

tholin: a molecule formed by the interaction of ultraviolet light and organic compounds such as methane and ethane.

tidally locked: when an object's orbital period matches its rotation, keeping one side facing the object it orbits.

tide: the daily rising and falling of large bodies of water, based on the pull of the moon's and sun's gravities.

toxic: poisonous, harmful, or deadly.

trans-Neptunian: objects, such as dwarf planets, whose orbit is beyond Neptune's orbit.

transit: when a smaller object, such as a planet, blocks a small amount of light from a star.

turbulent: unsteady or violent movement.

upper mantle: the part of the mantle closest to the crust.

vacuum: a space that is empty of matter.

vaporize: when a solid or liquid is turned directly into a gas, or vapor.

Venn diagram: a diagram that shows how things are related using circles that can overlap to show common traits.

volcanism: the motion of molten rock under the surface of a planet, which results in volcanos.

volume: a measure of how much space an object occupies.

Metric Conversions

Use this chart to find the metric equivalents to the English measurements in this activity. If you need to know a half measurement, divide by two. If you need to know twice the measurement, multiply by two.

English	Metric
1 inch	2.5 centimeters
1 foot	30.5 centimeters
1 yard	0.9 meter
1 mile	1.6 kilometers
1 pound	0.5 kilogram
1 teaspoon	5 milliliters
1 tablespoon	15 milliliters
1 cup	237 milliliters

RESOURCES

WEBSITES

Exoplanets
exoplanets.nasa.gov

Earth and Space Science for Younger Readers
spaceplace.nasa.gov
esa.int/esaKIDSen/Planetsandmoons.html

NASA's Solar System Guide
solarsystem.nasa.gov

Cassini Website (Saturn)
saturn.jpl.nasa.gov

Juno Website (Jupiter)
missionjuno.swri.edu

Curiosity (Mars)
mars.jpl.nasa.gov/msl

New Horizons (Pluto and the Kuiper Belt)
pluto.jhuapl.edu/index.php

The Search for Planet Nine
findplanetnine.com

Voyager Missions
voyager.jpl.nasa.gov

Rosetta and Philae (Comet 67p)
esa.int/Our_Activities/Space_Science/Rosetta

Psyche Mission (Asteroid Psyche)
jpl.nasa.gov/missions/psyche

Dawn Mission (Vesta and Ceres)
dawn.jpl.nasa.gov

QR CODE GLOSSARY

Page 8: nakedeyeplanets.com/visibility.htm#2016

Page 16: universetoday.com/48756/galileo-facts

Page 20: math.com/tables/geometry/volumes.htm

Page 24: universetoday.com/75843/why-are-there-seasons

Page 27: youtube.com/watch?v=X-dy4KEuso8

Page 29: youtube.com/watch?v=Xs0K4ApWl4g

Page 32: nasa.gov/feature/goddard/phobos-is-falling-apart

Page 34: mars.nasa.gov/msl

Page 36: exploratorium.edu/ronh/solar_system

Page 44: jpl.nasa.gov/missions/galileo

Page 47: youtube.com/watch?v=W1xUyJfd4dY

Page 54: npr.org/sections/thesalt/2017/03/10/519680335/saturn-s-pan-looks-more-like-a-pan-fried-dumpling-than-a-moon

Page 55: youtube.com/watch?v=HtYDPj6eFLc

Page 72: voyager.jpl.nasa.gov

Page 76: exploratorium.edu/ronh/solar_system

Page 79: neo.jpl.nasa.gov

Page 80: youtube.com/watch?v=r3Y-lPbjpPk

Page 83: deepspaceindustries.com/mining

Page 86: solarsystem.nasa.gov/planets/pluto/plutotime

Page 88: ourpluto.org/maps

Page 90: history.com/shows/the-universe/videos/shoemaker-levy-impact

Page 95: passc.net/EarthImpactDatabase/Worldmap.html

Page 95: simulator.down2earth.eu/planet.html?lang=en-US

Page 96: youtube.com/watch?v=FY_SFxP_jH0

Page 99: zooniverse.org/projects/marckuchner/backyard-worlds-planet-9

Page 102: exoplanets.nasa.gov/interactable/11

Page 104: nytimes.com/2016/10/04/science/hawaii-thirty-meter-telescope-mauna-kea.html?_r=0

Page 105: apod.nasa.gov/apod/ap170201.html

Page 106: wired.co.uk/article/nasa-nano-starship-breakthrough-starshot

Page 108: planethunters.org

INDEX

E

F

G

H

I

J

K

L

M

INDEX

R

S

T

INDEX